The UK
Tower Dual Basket Air Fryer
Cookbook for Beginners

Delicious and Guilt-Free Tower Air Fryer Recipes to Elevate Your Kitchen Game and Discover Culinary Magic | Full-Colour Edition

Patricia Albert

© Copyright 2024
- All Rights Reserved

This document is geared towards providing exact and reliable information concerning the topic and issue covered.

In no way is it legal to reproduce, duplicate, or transmit any part of this document in either electronic means or printed format. Recording this publication is strictly prohibited. Any storage of this document is not allowed unless with written permission from the publisher.

All rights reserved. The information provided herein is stated to be truthful and consistent, in that any liability, in terms of inattention or otherwise, by any usage or abuse of any policies, processes, or directions contained within is the solitary and utter responsibility of the recipient reader.

Under no circumstances will any legal responsibility or blame be held against the publisher for any reparation, damages, or monetary loss due to the information herein, either directly or indirectly. Respective authors own all copyrights not held by the publisher.

The information herein is offered for informational purposes solely and is universal as so. The presentation of the information is without a contract or any type of guarantee assurance. The trademarks used are without any consent, and the publication of any trademark is without permission or backing by the trademark owner.

All trademarks and brands within this book are for clarifying purposes only, are owned by the owners themselves, and are not affiliated with this document.

CONTENTS

❖ Introduction	01
❖ Fundamentals of Tower Dual Basket Air Fryer	02
❖ 4-Week Meal Plan	09

Week 1 09
Week 2 09
Week 3 10
Week 4 10

❖ Chapter 1 Breakfast	11

Egg in a Hole 11
White Whole Wheat Walnut Bread 11
Cheesy Ham and Tomato Sandwiches 12
Simple Breakfast Bread 12
Tofu Breakfast Sandwich 13
Ham, Apple, and Cheddar Panini 13
Christmas Pecan Eggnog Bread 14
Cheese and Vegetable Frittata 14
Banana Blueberry Oatmeal Bake 15
Butter Banana Bread 15
Bacon, Egg, and Cheese Breakfast Pockets 16
Perfect Cinnamon Rolls 17
Homemade Bagels 18

❖ Chapter 2 Vegetables and Sides	19

Roasted Lemon Broccoli 19
Smashed Potatoes with Yoghurt and Tomatoes 19
Crispy Shishito Tempura 20

Crispy Corn Croquettes	20
Orange Honey Glazed Carrots	21
Spicy Brussels Sprouts	21
Prosciutto Wrapped Asparagus	22
Air Fryer Potatoes with Onions and Peppers	22
Cabbage and Mushroom Spring Rolls	23
Crispy Sweet Potato Fries with Curry Yoghurt Dip	23
Cinnamon Sweet Potato Slices	24

❖ Chapter 3 Snacks and Starters 25

Crispy Lime Avocado Fries	25
Blooming Onion with Yum Yum Sauce	25
Bacon-Wrapped Dates	26
Mozzarella Sticks with Marinara Sauce	26
Rosemary Roasted Cashews	27
Spinach Artichoke Dip	27
Crunchy Chickpeas	28
Crispy Kale Chips	28
Cheesy Stuffed Mushrooms	29
Parmesan Cauliflower Cakes	29
Shrimp Potstickers	30
Crisp Root Vegetable Chips	30

❖ Chapter 4 Poultry 31

Honey-Lime Roasted Cornish Hen	31
Crispy Chicken Nuggets	31
Crispy Chicken Tenderloins	32
Italian Sausage Calzones	32
Italian Parmesan Chicken	33
Chicken Kabobs with Bell Peppers and Onions	33
Air Fryer Cajun Chicken Drumsticks	34
Buttermilk Fried Chicken Wings	34
Hot and Spicy Chicken Wings	35

Cheesy Chicken Taquitos	35
Turkey Cheeseburgers	36
Turkey and Rice Stuffed Poblano Peppers	36
Buffalo Chicken Drumettes	37
Herb Roasted Chicken Breast	37
Parmesan Chicken with Roasted Peanuts	38
Chinese Chicken with Broccoli	38
Homemade Nacho Chicken Strips	39

❖ Chapter 5 Fish and Seafood 40

Parmesan Cod Fillets with Spring Onion	40
Old Bay Tilapia Fillets	40
Crisp White Fish with Parsley	41
Salmon Croquettes	41
Air Fryer Shrimp Patties	42
Crispy Coconut Shrimp	42
Herbed Pollock with Olives and Tomatoes	43
Homemade Crunchy Shrimp	43
Basil Tilapia with Garlic Aioli	44
Spicy Lemon Shrimp	44
Lemon-Herb Salmon	45
Stuffed Courgettes with Cheesy Tuna	45
Dill Salmon Patties	46
Spicy Parmesan Tilapia	46
Lemon Butter Cod Fillets	47
Crispy Fish Sticks	47

❖ Chapter 6 Beef, Pork, and Lamb 48

Tender Rib Eye Steak	48
Savoury Meat Loaf	48
Air Fryer Steak Bites with Mushrooms	49
Simple Beef Roast	49
BBQ Pulled Pork Empanadas	50

Spiced Sirloin Steak 50

Spicy Garlic Lamb Chops 51

Beef Steak Fajita Tacos 51

Crispy Pork Belly 52

Easy Air Fried Hot Dogs 52

Beef Satay with Peanut Sauce 53

Curried Lime Pork Satay 53

Pork Burgers 54

The Best Meatballs 54

Meatballs with Creamy Gravy 55

Delicious Turkish Pizza 56

Cheese Beef Lasagna 57

Flavourful Vietnamese Roasted Pork 58

❖ Chapter 7 Desserts 59

Homemade Gingerbread 59

Doughnuts with Chocolate Sauce 59

Cinnamon Doughnut Holes 60

Air Fried Pineapple Rings with Almonds 60

Sweet Coconut Rice Cake 61

Classic Banana Bundt Cake 61

Fig and Almond Hand Pies 62

Crispy Bananas with Chocolate Sauce 62

Chocolate Bundt Cake 63

Easy Blueberry Crisp 63

Fudge Brownies 64

Conclusion 65

Appendix Recipes Index 66

Introduction

Welcome to the UK Tower Dual Basket Air Fryer Cookbook, your comprehensive guide to mastering the art of air frying with the versatile Tower Dual Basket Air Fryer. Designed for home cooks of all skill levels, this cookbook showcases a variety of delicious, easy-to-make recipes that not only promote healthier cooking but also maximise the unique features of your Tower air fryer.

With the dual basket feature, you can cook two different dishes simultaneously, allowing you to prepare complete meals in less time. This book is filled with mouthwatering recipes that take full advantage of this innovative appliance, offering you the convenience of preparing healthier meals with minimal oil, while still achieving that delicious crispy texture you love. Whether you're cooking for yourself, your family, or guests, these recipes are designed to be simple, quick, and satisfying.

From hearty breakfasts and quick snacks to mains and sides, every recipe is paired with beautiful, full-colour pictures to inspire and guide you through the cooking process. Each dish is carefully crafted to ensure balanced nutrition, making it easier to enjoy guilt-free meals without compromising on taste.

In addition to a wide array of recipes, this cookbook provides helpful tips and tricks for getting the most out of your Tower Dual Basket Air Fryer. You'll learn how to cook with confidence while saving time and energy. Discover a new way of cooking with this essential guide and start creating healthier, tastier meals that the whole family will enjoy. Start your cooking with the Tower Dual Basket Air Fryer!

Fundamentals of Tower Dual Basket Air Fryer

The Tower Dual Basket Air Fryer offers a convenient and efficient way to prepare healthier meals without compromising on taste. Featuring innovative dual-basket technology, this air fryer allows you to cook two different dishes simultaneously, saving you valuable time in the kitchen. With its adjustable temperature control and various cooking presets, you can easily achieve perfect results for a wide range of foods, from crispy chips to succulent chicken.

The fryer uses rapid air circulation to ensure even cooking and a deliciously crispy texture, while significantly reducing the need for oil compared to traditional frying methods. The non-stick, dishwasher-safe drawers make for effortless cleaning, ensuring that maintaining your appliance is hassle-free. Compact and stylish, the Tower Dual Basket Air Fryer is an ideal addition to any kitchen, perfect for busy families looking to enjoy healthier meals without the fuss. Embrace a smarter cooking experience with this versatile kitchen essential.

What is Tower Dual Basket Air Fryer?

The Tower Dual Basket Air Fryer is a cutting-edge kitchen appliance designed to revolutionise the way you prepare meals at home. This innovative air fryer utilises advanced rapid air circulation technology to deliver deliciously crispy results with significantly less oil than traditional frying methods, making it a healthier alternative for cooking your favourite dishes.

What sets the Tower Dual Basket Air Fryer apart from conventional models is its unique dual-basket feature, which allows you to cook two separate dishes simultaneously. This not only saves you time but also makes it easier to prepare complete meals in one go. With its large capacity, you can cater to the needs of busy families or entertaining guests without the hassle of multiple cooking sessions.

Equipped with adjustable temperature controls and various pre-set cooking functions, the Tower Dual Basket Air Fryer provides versatility in cooking. Whether you're frying, baking, roasting, or grilling, this appliance can handle it all, ensuring perfectly cooked food every time. The intuitive digital display makes it easy to select your desired settings and monitor the cooking progress, enhancing your overall cooking experience. Here are the control panel of this appliance.

Control Panel:

1. **Drawer 1 Key:** This button displays the status of Drawer 1.
2. **Drawer 2 Key:** This button displays the status of Drawer 2.
3. **Temperature Indicator:** This shows the current temperature setting.
4. **Temperature + Key:** Use this button to increase the temperature.
5. **Temperature – Key:** Use this button to decrease the temperature.
6. **LED Screen:** This displays the basic cooking time.
7. **Time Indicator:** This shows the current time setting.
8. **Time + Key:** Use this button to increase the cooking time.
9. **Time – Key:** Use this button to decrease the cooking time.
10. **Drawer 1 Light Key:** This button turns the internal light on or off in Drawer 1. Press to activate the light for better visibility of the food, and press again to turn it off.
11. **Drawer 2 Light Key:** This button turns the internal light on or off in Drawer 2. Press to activate the light for better visibility of the food, and

press again to turn it off.

12. Power On/Off Button: This button turns the air fryer on or off. Press to activate, and hold to turn it off.
13. Start/Pause Key: This allows you to start or stop cooking. After setting the time and temperature, press to begin cooking, and press again to pause.
14. Pre-Heat Key: Prepares the air fryer to the optimal cooking temperature. Press to preheat, and a notification will display when it's ready.
15. Chips Pre-set Key: Automatically selects the ideal temperature and time for cooking chips. Press to set the air fryer for chips.
16. Drumsticks Pre-set Key: Automatically selects the best cooking settings for chicken drumsticks. Press to set the air fryer for drumsticks.
17. Steak Pre-set Key: Automatically determines the perfect cooking time and temperature for steaks. Press to set the air fryer for steaks.
18. Cake Pre-set Key: Automatically selects the ideal settings for baking cakes. Press to set the air fryer for cakes.
19. Smart Finish Key: Synchronises the cooking times of both baskets to finish at the same time. Press to ensure both baskets complete cooking together.
20. Match Cook Key: Aligns cooking parameters between both baskets. Press to apply the same settings to both baskets for consistent results.
21. Prawn Pre-set Key: Automatically sets the perfect cooking time and temperature for prawns. Press to configure the air fryer for prawns.
22. Fish Pre-set Key: Automatically sets the cooking time and temperature for fish. Press to configure the air fryer for fish.
23. Pizza Pre-Set Key: Automatically determines the ideal settings for cooking pizza. Press to configure the air fryer for pizza.
24. Vegetables Pre-set Key: Automatically selects the best cooking time and temperature for vegetables. Press to set the air fryer for vegetables.
25. Dehydrate Pre-set Key: Automatically determines the right settings for dehydrating fruits, vegetables, and meats. Press to configure the air fryer for dehydration.

Also, cleaning the Tower Dual Basket Air Fryer is a breeze, thanks to its non-stick, dishwasher-safe drawers and grill plates. This means you can spend less time cleaning up and more time enjoying your delicious creations. Additionally, the sleek and modern design of the air fryer ensures that it will complement any kitchen decor.

In summary, the Tower Dual Basket Air Fryer combines functionality, convenience, and health-conscious cooking into one powerful appliance. With its ability to prepare two dishes at once, adjustable settings, and easy cleanup, it is an essential tool for anyone looking to enjoy healthier, home-cooked meals without sacrificing flavour or texture. Embrace the future of cooking with the Tower Dual Basket Air Fryer and elevate your culinary skills today.

Benefits of Using It

The Tower Dual Basket Air Fryer is a revolutionary kitchen appliance that offers a multitude of benefits for those looking to simplify their cooking process while maintaining a healthy lifestyle. Here's a detailed look at ten significant advantages of using this versatile air fryer.

1. Healthier Cooking
One of the most notable benefits of the Tower Dual Basket Air Fryer is its ability to prepare meals with significantly less oil compared to traditional frying methods. Using rapid air circulation technology, this appliance allows you to achieve the same crispy texture and flavour without the excess fat, making it an excellent choice for health-conscious individuals and families.

2. Dual-Basket Convenience
The unique dual-basket feature sets this air fryer apart from others on the market. With two separate cooking compartments, you can prepare two different dishes simultaneously. This saves time and energy, particularly when cooking for larger gatherings or busy families. You can whip up a complete meal—such as chicken in one basket and vegetables in the other—without any hassle.

3. Versatile Cooking Options
The Tower Dual Basket Air Fryer is not limited to just frying. It offers multiple cooking functions, allowing you to enjoy many delicious meals. This versatility makes it an all-in-one kitchen appliance that can handle various recipes, from crispy fries to delectable cakes, making it suitable for any meal of the day.

4. Consistent Cooking Results
Equipped with precise temperature controls and various pre-set functions, this air fryer ensures consistent cooking results every time. You can trust that your food will be evenly cooked and perfectly browned, eliminating the guesswork often associated with traditional frying or baking.

5. User-Friendly Interface
The Tower Dual Basket Air Fryer features an intuitive digital control panel, making it easy for users to select their desired settings. With clear displays and simple buttons, even novice cooks can navigate the appliance without difficulty. This accessibility encourages more people to explore healthy cooking.

6. Easy Cleanup
Cleaning up after cooking can be one of the most tedious tasks in the kitchen. The Tower Dual Basket Air Fryer simplifies this process with its non-stick, dishwasher-safe baskets. You can easily remove and wash them after use, ensuring that your appliance remains in excellent condition without extensive scrubbing.

7. Energy Efficiency
This air fryer is designed with energy efficiency in mind. Unlike traditional ovens that take time to preheat and consume more energy, the Tower Dual Basket Air Fryer heats up quickly and cooks food faster. This not only reduces energy consumption but also allows you to prepare

meals more quickly, saving you both time and money on utility bills.

8. Compact Design
The Tower Dual Basket Air Fryer features a compact design that is perfect for kitchens with limited counter space. Its sleek appearance makes it an attractive addition to your kitchen, and its lightweight nature allows for easy storage when not in use. This space-saving feature makes it accessible for everyone, from students in small apartments to families in larger homes.

9. Enhanced Flavour
The air frying process enhances the natural flavours of your ingredients. Since the appliance uses less oil, the food retains its natural juices and textures, providing a more authentic taste experience. Additionally, the ability to season food freely without the fear of excess oil allows for greater culinary creativity.

10. Family-Friendly Cooking
With the growing trend of healthy eating, the Tower Dual Basket Air Fryer makes it easier to prepare nutritious meals that the whole family will love. Its ability to cook a variety of dishes simultaneously encourages families to sit down together and enjoy home-cooked meals. Moreover, children can be involved in the cooking process, learning about healthier food choices and cooking techniques in a fun and engaging way.

In conclusion, the Tower Dual Basket Air Fryer offers numerous benefits that make it an invaluable addition to any kitchen. From promoting healthier eating habits and providing versatile cooking options to simplifying cleanup and enhancing flavour, this appliance is designed to cater to the modern home cook's needs. Whether you're preparing a quick dinner for one or a feast for the entire family, the Tower Dual Basket Air Fryer helps you do it all with ease and efficiency. Embrace the convenience and health advantages of air frying today and elevate your culinary experiences with this innovative appliance.

Before First Use

Before using your appliance for the first time, it is essential to read all instructions and safety information meticulously. Retaining this information will ensure you have it for future reference. Please follow the steps outlined below:

1. Unpack the Appliance: Carefully remove your appliance from its packaging, ensuring you do so gently to avoid any accidental damage.

2. Inspect for Damage: Examine the cord for any signs of wear or damage. Additionally, check the body of the appliance for any visible defects or blemishes that may have occurred during shipping.

3. Responsible Disposal: Dispose of the packaging materials in an environmentally responsible manner. Consider recycling where possible to minimise waste.

4. Remove Stickers and Labels: Carefully peel off any stickers or labels that may be affixed to the appliance. However, ensure that the rating label remains intact, as it contains important information regarding the appliance's specifications.

5. Clean the Components: Thoroughly clean the grill plates, baskets, and drawers using hot water mixed with a mild washing-up liquid. Utilise a non-abrasive sponge to prevent scratches. After cleaning, ensure all components are dried thoroughly to avoid any moisture buildup.

6. Install Grill Plates: Before you begin using the appliance, place the grill plates securely in the bottom of the drawers to prepare for cooking.

7. Wipe the Appliance: Using a damp cloth, wipe both the inside and outside surfaces of the appliance. Ensure that you dry it thoroughly afterwards to maintain its appearance and functionality.

8. Avoid Using Oil or Fat: It is crucial not to fill the appliance with oil or frying fat, as this appliance is designed to operate using hot air. It requires very little to no oil for effective cooking.

9. Familiarise with the Control Panel: Take the time to understand the control panel features as detailed in the Specifications section of your

manual. Familiarity will enhance your cooking experience.
10. Proper Placement: Position your appliance in accordance with the Important Safety Instructions section to ensure optimal safety and performance during use.

By adhering to these guidelines, you will ensure the safe and effective use of your appliance, allowing you to enjoy its full benefits while cooking.

Step-By-Step Guide to Tower Dual Basket Air Fryer

Air Fryer Drawer Safety Switch

The air fryer is equipped with a safety switch located in the drawer to prevent accidental activation when the drawer is not correctly positioned or the timer is unset. Before use, ensure that the grill plate is inside the drawer and that the drawer is fully closed.

Removing the Drawer:
• The drawer can be completely removed from the air fryer. To do this, simply pull on the handle to slide the drawer out. (Note: If the drawer is removed while the air fryer is in operation, the unit will automatically stop. All indicator lights will turn off, and when the drawer is replaced, the fryer will resume with the last selected settings.)

The Auto-Off Function:
• If no interaction occurs with the control panel for 10 minutes while cooking is inactive, the appliance will turn off automatically. (Note: To manually turn off the unit during operation, press the ON/Standby key. The key will flash, the unit will stop heating, and the fan will run for about 10 seconds before shutting down completely. An audible signal will sound, and the ON/Standby icon will remain lit.)

Turning the Appliance ON/OFF:
• Plug the unit into a mains socket. You will hear an audible signal, and the control panel will briefly illuminate before entering standby mode, where only the Power key will be lit.
• Touch the Power key to activate the appliance, illuminating the control panel.
• To stop further operation, touch the Power key again. The unit will emit a signal and enter standby mode. (Note: In case of a power cut or if the unit is unplugged during operation, all indicator lights will turn off. Once power is restored, the unit will continue operating with the previously set program.)

Start/Pause Function:
• After setting the desired function, time, and temperature, touch the Start/Pause key.
• The Start/Pause key will flash and emit an audible signal before the unit begins its cooking program.
• To pause operation, press the Start/Pause key again. The key will stop flashing, and you will hear a signal. Press the Start/Pause key once more to resume operation at the last setting.

Setting the Temperature:
• The temperature can be adjusted between 50-200°C.
• Each press of the Temperature +/- keys will increase or decrease the temperature in increments of 10°C, and the display will flash three times to confirm the selected setting. (Note: When the temperature reaches 200°C and the Temperature + key is pressed, the display will loop back to 50°C. Conversely, pressing the Temperature - key at 50°C will cycle back to 200°C.)
• Short press the keys for gradual adjustment, or press and hold for quicker changes. (Note: The temperature can be adjusted during operation.)

Setting the Timer:
• The timer can be set for a duration of 1 to 60 minutes.
• Each press of the Timer +/- keys will increase or decrease the time by 1 minute. (Note: When the timer reaches 60 minutes and the key is pressed again, it will loop back to 01 minute. Pressing the key at 01 minute will cycle

back to 60 minutes. The display will flash three times to confirm the chosen setting. Use short presses for gradual changes or press and hold for rapid adjustments. The timer can also be changed while the unit is in operation.)

Pre-Set Menu Selection
Once the appliance is plugged in and in standby mode:

1. Load the Food: Place the food into the drawer(s). Caution: Do not exceed the maximum fill line.
2. Power On: Press the Power key to turn the appliance on.
3. Select Drawer: Press the drawer 1 or drawer 2 key, depending on which drawer contains food.
4. Choose Cooking Function: Tap the icon of the desired cooking function.
5. Adjust Settings: The default temperature and timer will display alternately. Use the Temperature + / - keys and the Time + / - keys to adjust if necessary.
6. For Both Drawers: If using both drawers, press the key for the other drawer and repeat steps 3 and 4.
7. Start Cooking: Press the Start/Pause key to commence operation.
8. End of Cooking: When the timer reaches zero, an audible signal will sound, the display will show '00', and the heating element will stop. The motor will continue running for about 1 minute to cool down before entering standby mode.
9. Remove the Drawer: Carefully take the drawer out of the appliance and place it on a heat-resistant surface.
10. Check Food Readiness:
• If the food is undercooked, return the drawer to the appliance, set a few extra minutes on the timer, and press the Start/Pause key.
• If the food is ready, empty the drawer into a bowl or onto a plate. Caution: Tilt the drawer carefully, as any excess oil collected at the bottom may spill onto the food.

Important Notes:

• Be cautious when tilting the drawer, as the grill plate may shift.
• Avoid touching the drawer during and shortly after use, as it becomes very hot. Always hold the drawer by the handle.
• Once a batch of food is ready, the appliance is ready for another batch. If no further cooking is required, turn off the appliance and unplug it from the mains socket. Leave the drawer(s) open to help cool the unit more quickly.

Smart Finish
1. Program Drawer 1: Set up the desired cooking program for drawer 1.
2. Program Drawer 2: Set the cooking program for drawer 2 accordingly.
3. Select Smart Finish: Choose the Smart Finish option to coordinate the cooking times.
4. Start Cooking: Press the Start/Pause key to initiate the cooking process.
5. End of Cooking: Remove and enjoy.

Match Cook
If cooking the same food in both drawers, set the program for drawer 1 as detailed above
and then MATCH COOK drawer 2.

1. Select MATCH COOK: Choose the Match Cook option to cook the same food.
2. Program drawer 1: Set up the desired cooking program for drawer 1.
3. Start Cooking: Press the Start/Pause key to initiate the cooking process.
4. End of Cooking: Remove and enjoy.

Pre-Heat
To prepare the appliance for cooking, it is advisable to pre-heat:
1. Select Drawer(s): Choose either the required drawer or both for pre-heating.
2. Choose Pre-Heat Function: Press the Pre-Heat function button, which will pre-heat the selected drawer at 180ºC for 3 minutes.

3.Initiate Pre-Heating: Press the Start/Pause key to start the pre-heating process.
Note: Pre-heating the grill plate is beneficial for achieving a chargrill effect when cooking vegetables, chicken, meat, and fish. It also adds extra crispness to chips and other coated ingredients.

Helpful Cooking Tips

Here are some tips for you to maximize your use of Tower Dual Basket Air Fryer.
1.Shake Ingredients: Shake smaller ingredients halfway through the cooking time to ensure an even fry and improve the final result.
2.Parboil Potatoes: For fluffy fries, it's advisable to parboil the potatoes before frying.
3.Use Oil for Crispiness: Add a little oil to fresh potatoes to achieve a crispy texture. Fry the ingredients shortly after adding the oil for the best results.
4.Ideal Quantity for Fries: The best amount for making crispy fries is 500 grams.
5.Caution with Greasy Foods: Be careful when using very greasy ingredients, such as sausages, in the air fryer.
6.Versatile Snacks: Snacks that are typically baked in the oven can also be cooked in the air fryer.
7.Pre-Made Dough: Use pre-made dough for quick and easy filled snacks, as it requires less cooking time compared to homemade dough.
8.Use Baking Tins: If you wish to bake a cake or quiche, or fry delicate or filled ingredients, place a baking tin or oven dish in the air fryer basket.
9.Reheating Food: The air fryer can be used to reheat food; simply select the reheat function.

Cleaning and Caring for Tower Dual Basket Air Fryer

1.Unplug the Appliance: Before cleaning your Tower Dual Basket Air Fryer, ensure it is unplugged from the mains socket and has cooled down completely. This is essential for your safety.

2.Remove the Drawers and Grill Plates: Carefully detach the baskets and drawers from the air fryer. These components are usually dishwasher safe, making cleaning easier.
3.Clean the Drawers and Grill Plates:
• **Hand Wash:** Use warm, soapy water and a non-abrasive sponge to clean the drawers and grill plates. Avoid using harsh scrubbers that may scratch the non-stick surface.
• **Dishwasher Safe:** If you prefer, you can place the drawers and grill plates in the dishwasher. Ensure they are positioned securely to avoid any damage during the wash cycle.
4.Wipe the Exterior: Use a damp cloth to wipe down the exterior of the air fryer. A mild detergent can be used if there are stubborn stains. Avoid using abrasive cleaners or solvents as they can damage the finish.
5.Clean the Heating Element:
• **Avoid Water Contact:** Do not immerse the heating element in water. Instead, use a soft, dry cloth to wipe away any food residues.
• **Inspect for Buildup:** Regularly check the heating element for any grease or food buildup. Keeping it clean ensures optimal cooking performance.
6.Remove Food Residues: After each use, inspect the interior of the air fryer for any leftover food particles or grease. Wipe them away with a damp cloth to prevent build-up.
7.Odour Removal: If you notice any lingering odours, mix equal parts of water and vinegar in a bowl and place it in the air fryer basket. Run the air fryer at a low temperature for a few minutes to help neutralise the smells.
8.Check for Damage: Regularly inspect the baskets, drawers, and appliance for any signs of wear or damage. If you notice any cracks or peeling, discontinue use and contact customer service for replacement parts.
9.Store Properly: Once cleaned and dried, store the air fryer in a cool, dry place. Ensure that the baskets and drawers are placed back in the appliance to keep it compact.
By following these cleaning and care tips, you can ensure that your

Tower Dual Basket Air Fryer remains in excellent condition, providing you with delicious, healthier meals for years to come.

Frequently Asked Questions

1. What is the capacity of the Tower Dual Basket Air Fryer?
The Tower Dual Basket Air Fryer typically has a combined capacity of 10 litres, allowing you to cook multiple portions at once, making it ideal for families or gatherings.

2. How does the dual basket feature work?
The dual basket feature allows you to cook different foods simultaneously at varying temperatures and times. This means you can prepare a complete meal without having to wait for one item to finish cooking before starting another.

3. Is the Tower Dual Basket Air Fryer easy to clean?
Yes, the air fryer is designed with easy-clean drawers and grill plates that are dishwasher safe. Additionally, the non-stick surfaces help reduce food residue, making hand washing straightforward.

4. Can I use oil in the air fryer?
While the air fryer requires very little oil compared to traditional frying methods, you can add a small amount of oil to enhance crispiness, especially for items like fries or roasted vegetables.

5. What types of food can I cook in the air fryer?
The Tower Dual Basket Air Fryer is versatile and can be used to prepare a wide variety of foods, including chips, chicken, fish, vegetables, and even baked goods like cakes and pastries.

6. Does the air fryer require preheating?
Preheating is not strictly necessary, but doing so can improve cooking results. If you choose to preheat, simply select the preheat function and allow it to reach the desired temperature before adding your food.

7. Is the air fryer safe to use?
Yes, the Tower Dual Basket Air Fryer includes multiple safety features, such as a cool-touch exterior, automatic shut-off, and a safety switch in the drawer to prevent accidental operation when the drawer is not correctly in place.

8. Can I cook different types of food in each basket simultaneously?
Yes, the Tower Dual Basket Air Fryer allows you to cook different types of food in each basket at the same time. The Smart Finish feature ensures that both dishes finish cooking simultaneously, even if they have different cooking times. This versatility makes it perfect for preparing a complete meal efficiently.

9. How do I know when my food is done cooking?
The Tower Dual Basket Air Fryer features a timer and temperature indicator that will alert you when the cooking time has elapsed. Additionally, it's recommended to check the food's doneness halfway through the cooking process by shaking or stirring, ensuring even cooking.

10. What should I do if my air fryer is smoking?
If you notice smoke coming from your air fryer, it may be due to excess oil or food particles that have accumulated. To resolve this, ensure that the baskets are clean and free of leftover residues. If necessary, reduce the amount of oil used, and always monitor cooking times to prevent burning.

4-Week Meal Plan

Week 1

Day 1:
Breakfast: Cheese and Vegetable Frittata
Lunch: Crispy Shishito Tempura
Snack: Bacon-Wrapped Dates
Dinner: Honey-Lime Roasted Cornish Hen
Dessert: Homemade Gingerbread

Day 2:
Breakfast: Bacon, Egg, and Cheese Breakfast Pockets
Lunch: Smashed Potatoes with Yoghurt and Tomatoes
Snack: Mozzarella Sticks with Marinara Sauce
Dinner: Salmon Croquettes
Dessert: Doughnuts with Chocolate Sauce

Day 3:
Breakfast: Egg in a Hole
Lunch: Roasted Lemon Broccoli
Snack: Blooming Onion with Yum Yum Sauce
Dinner: Meatballs with Creamy Gravy
Dessert: Sweet Coconut Rice Cake

Day 4:
Breakfast: White Whole Wheat Walnut Bread
Lunch: Crispy Corn Croquettes
Snack: Crunchy Chickpeas
Dinner: Homemade Nacho Chicken Strips
Dessert: Easy Blueberry Crisp

Day 5:
Breakfast: Perfect Cinnamon Rolls
Lunch: Orange Honey Glazed Carrots
Snack: Crispy Lime Avocado Fries
Dinner: Parmesan Cod Fillets with Spring Onion
Dessert: Fig and Almond Hand Pies

Day 6:
Breakfast: Cheesy Ham and Tomato Sandwiches
Lunch: Spicy Brussels Sprouts
Snack: Crispy Kale Chips
Dinner: Cheese Beef Lasagna
Dessert: Classic Banana Bundt Cake

Day 7:
Breakfast: Simple Breakfast Bread
Lunch: Prosciutto Wrapped Asparagus
Snack: Rosemary Roasted Cashews
Dinner: Flavourful Vietnamese Roasted Pork
Dessert: Air Fried Pineapple Rings with Almonds

Week 2

Day 1:
Breakfast: Tofu Breakfast Sandwich
Lunch: Air Fryer Potatoes with Onions and Peppers
Snack: Spinach Artichoke Dip
Dinner: Italian Parmesan Chicken
Dessert: Cinnamon Doughnut Holes

Day 2:
Breakfast: Ham, Apple, and Cheddar Panini
Lunch: Cabbage and Mushroom Spring Rolls
Snack: Shrimp Potstickers
Dinner: Herbed Pollock with Olives and Tomatoes
Dessert: Crispy Bananas with Chocolate Sauce

Day 3:
Breakfast: Banana Blueberry Oatmeal Bake
Lunch: Crispy Sweet Potato Fries with Curry Yoghurt Dip
Snack: Crisp Root Vegetable Chips
Dinner: Savoury Meat Loaf
Dessert: Fudge Brownies

Day 4:
Breakfast: Butter Banana Bread
Lunch: Cinnamon Sweet Potato Slices
Snack: Cheesy Stuffed Mushrooms
Dinner: Buttermilk Fried Chicken Wings
Dessert: Homemade Gingerbread

Day 5:
Breakfast: Homemade Bagels
Lunch: Crispy Shishito Tempura
Snack: Parmesan Cauliflower Cakes
Dinner: Crispy Coconut Shrimp
Dessert: Chocolate Bundt Cake

Day 6:
Breakfast: Bacon, Egg, and Cheese Breakfast Pockets
Lunch: Smashed Potatoes with Yoghurt and Tomatoes
Snack: Bacon-Wrapped Dates
Dinner: Spiced Sirloin Steak
Dessert: Doughnuts with Chocolate Sauce

Day 7:
Breakfast: Egg in a Hole
Lunch: Roasted Lemon Broccoli
Snack: Mozzarella Sticks with Marinara Sauce
Dinner: Spicy Garlic Lamb Chops
Dessert: Sweet Coconut Rice Cake

Week 3

Day 1:
Breakfast: White Whole Wheat Walnut Bread
Lunch: Crispy Corn Croquettes
Snack: Blooming Onion with Yum Yum Sauce
Dinner: Turkey Cheeseburgers
Dessert: Cinnamon Doughnut Holes

Day 2:
Breakfast: Cheesy Ham and Tomato Sandwiches
Lunch: Orange Honey Glazed Carrots
Snack: Crispy Lime Avocado Fries
Dinner: Basil Tilapia with Garlic Aioli
Dessert: Classic Banana Bundt Cake

Day 3:
Breakfast: Cheese and Vegetable Frittata
Lunch: Spicy Brussels Sprouts
Snack: Crunchy Chickpeas
Dinner: Beef Steak Fajita Tacos
Dessert: Air Fried Pineapple Rings with Almonds

Day 4:
Breakfast: Perfect Cinnamon Rolls
Lunch: Prosciutto Wrapped Asparagus
Snack: Crispy Kale Chips
Dinner: Italian Sausage Calzones
Dessert: Easy Blueberry Crisp

Day 5:
Breakfast: Christmas Pecan Eggnog Bread
Lunch: Air Fryer Potatoes with Onions and Peppers
Snack: Rosemary Roasted Cashews
Dinner: Lemon Butter Cod Fillets
Dessert: Chocolate Bundt Cake

Day 6:
Breakfast: Tofu Breakfast Sandwich
Lunch: Cabbage and Mushroom Spring Rolls
Snack: Spinach Artichoke Dip
Dinner: Beef Satay with Peanut Sauce
Dessert: Fig and Almond Hand Pies

Day 7:
Breakfast: Ham, Apple, and Cheddar Panini
Lunch: Crispy Sweet Potato Fries with Curry Yoghurt Dip
Snack: Shrimp Potstickers
Dinner: Crispy Pork Belly
Dessert: Crispy Bananas with Chocolate Sauce

Week 4

Day 1:
Breakfast: Simple Breakfast Bread
Lunch: Cinnamon Sweet Potato Slices
Snack: Crisp Root Vegetable Chips
Dinner: Turkey and Rice Stuffed Poblano Peppers
Dessert: Fudge Brownies

Day 2:
Breakfast: Banana Blueberry Oatmeal Bake
Lunch: Crispy Shishito Tempura
Snack: Cheesy Stuffed Mushrooms
Dinner: Spicy Lemon Shrimp
Dessert: Homemade Gingerbread

Day 3:
Breakfast: Butter Banana Bread
Lunch: Smashed Potatoes with Yoghurt and Tomatoes
Snack: Parmesan Cauliflower Cakes
Dinner: The Best Meatballs
Dessert: Doughnuts with Chocolate Sauce

Day 4:
Breakfast: Bacon, Egg, and Cheese Breakfast Pockets
Lunch: Roasted Lemon Broccoli
Snack: Bacon-Wrapped Dates
Dinner: Air Fryer Cajun Chicken Drumsticks
Dessert: Sweet Coconut Rice Cake

Day 5:
Breakfast: Homemade Bagels
Lunch: Crispy Corn Croquettes
Snack: Mozzarella Sticks with Marinara Sauce
Dinner: Spicy Parmesan Tilapia
Dessert: Cinnamon Doughnut Holes

Day 6:
Breakfast: Egg in a Hole
Lunch: Orange Honey Glazed Carrots
Snack: Blooming Onion with Yum Yum Sauce
Dinner: Tender Rib Eye Steak
Dessert: Air Fried Pineapple Rings with Almonds

Day 7:
Breakfast: Cheese and Vegetable Frittata
Lunch: Spicy Brussels Sprouts
Snack: Crispy Lime Avocado Fries
Dinner: Curried Lime Pork Satay
Dessert: Classic Banana Bundt Cake

Chapter 1 Breakfast

Egg in a Hole

⏱ **Prep: 5 minutes** 🍳 **Cook: 6 minutes** 📚 **Serves: 1**

Ingredients:

1 slice bread
1 teaspoon soft butter
1 egg
Salt and pepper
1 tablespoon shredded Cheddar cheese
2 teaspoons diced ham

Preparation:

1. Place a round baking dish inside one drawer. 2. Using a 2½-inch-diameter biscuit cutter, cut a hole in the centre of the bread slice. 3. Spread softened butter on both sides of bread. 4. Lay bread slice in a baking dish and crack an egg into the hole. Sprinkle egg with salt and pepper to taste. 5. Cook at 165°C for 5 minutes. 6. Flip the toast and sprinkle it with shredded cheese and diced ham. Cook for an additional 1 to 2 minutes or until the yolk is cooked to your preference.

White Whole Wheat Walnut Bread

⏱ **Prep: 25 minutes** 🍳 **Cook: 20 minutes** 📚 **Serves: 8**

Ingredients:

235ml lukewarm water (40–45°C)
1 packet instant yeast
1 tablespoon light brown sugar
250g whole-grain white wheat flour
1 egg, room temperature, beaten with a fork
2 teaspoons olive oil
½ teaspoon salt
60g chopped walnuts
Cooking spray

Preparation:

1. In a small bowl, mix the water, yeast, and brown sugar. 2. Pour yeast mixture over flour and mix until smooth. 3. Add the egg, olive oil, and salt and beat with a wooden spoon for about 2 minutes. 4. Stir in chopped walnuts. You will have very thick batter rather than stiff bread dough. 5. Spray air fryer baking pan with cooking spray and pour in batter, smoothing the top. 6. Let the batter rise for 15 minutes. 7. Cook bread at 180°C for 20 to 25 minutes, until a toothpick pushed into the centre comes out with crumbs clinging. Let bread rest for 10 minutes before removing from the pan.

Cheesy Ham and Tomato Sandwiches

⏰ **Prep: 5 minutes**   🍲 **Cook: 8 minutes**   ❖ **Serves: 2**

❯ **Ingredients:**

1 teaspoon butter
4 slices bread
4 slices smoked country ham
4 slices Cheddar cheese
4 thick slices tomato

❯ **Preparation:**

1. Spread ½ teaspoon of butter onto one side of 2 slices of bread. Each sandwich will have 1 slice of bread with butter and 1 slice without. 2. Assemble each sandwich by layering 2 slices of ham, 2 slices of cheese, and 2 slices of tomato on the unbuttered pieces of bread. Top with the other bread slices, buttered side up. 3. Place the sandwiches in the air fryer drawer buttered-side down. Cook at 185°C for 4 minutes. 4. Open the air fryer. Flip the grilled cheese sandwiches. Cook for an additional 4 minutes. 5. Cool before serving. Cut each sandwich in half and enjoy.

Simple Breakfast Bread

⏰ **Prep: 15 minutes**   🍲 **Cook: 5 minutes**   ❖ **Serves: 4**

❯ **Ingredients:**

125g flour
2 teaspoons baking powder
¼ teaspoon salt
60ml lukewarm milk
1 teaspoon oil
2–3 tablespoons water
Oil for misting or cooking spray

❯ **Preparation:**

1. Stir together flour, baking powder, and salt. Gently mix in the milk and oil. Stir in 1 tablespoon water. If needed, add more water, 1 tablespoon at a time, until stiff dough forms. The dough shouldn't be sticky, so use only as much as you need. 2. Divide dough into 4 portions and shape into balls. Cover with a towel and let rest for 10 minutes. 3. Pat thinner into rectangles about 3 x 6 inches. This will create a thinner bread to serve as a base for dishes such as Indian tacos. 4. Spray both sides of dough pieces with oil or cooking spray. 5. Place the dough rectangles in each air fryer drawer and select the Match Cook setting. Cook at 200°C for 3 minutes. Spray tops, turn, spray the other side, and cook for 2 more minutes. If necessary, repeat to cook the remaining bread. 6. Serve piping hot as is or allow to cool slightly and add toppings to create your own Native American tacos.

Chapter 1 Breakfast

Tofu Breakfast Sandwich

⏱ Prep: 15 minutes   🍳 Cook: 13 minutes   🍽 Serves: 2

Ingredients:

1 (225g) package firm or extra-firm tofu, thinly sliced into rectangles or squares
2 teaspoons nutritional yeast, divided
¼ teaspoon sea salt, divided
⅛ teaspoon freshly ground black pepper, divided
Cooking oil spray (sunflower, safflower, or refined coconut)
4 slices bread
Cheesy sauce
Vegan tempeh bacon (optional)
Vegan mayo, your choice (optional)
Leaf lettuce, dill pickles, and thinly sliced red onion (optional)

Preparation:

1. Place the tofu slices in one layer on a plate and sprinkle evenly with 1 teaspoon nutritional yeast, ⅛ teaspoon salt, and half of the black pepper. Turn over and sprinkle the remaining yeast, salt, and pepper on top. 2. Spray the air fryer drawer with the oil and place the tofu pieces in a single layer in the drawer. Spray the tops with the oil. Bake at 200°C for 7 minutes. 3. While the tofu is cooking, prepare your optional additions. 4. After the tofu has cooked for 7 minutes, flip each piece over and spray again with oil. Bake for an additional 6 minutes or until golden and lightly crisp. 5. Toast the bread, and top with the tofu slices, Cheesy Sauce, vegan meat (if using), and any additional toppings. Devour immediately.

Ham, Apple, and Cheddar Panini

⏱ Prep: 10 minutes   🍳 Cook: 5 minutes   🍽 Serves: 4

Ingredients:

2 slices whole grain bread
2 teaspoons Dijon mustard
2 thin slices low-fat cheddar cheese
30g thinly sliced cooked low-sodium ham
3 thin slices Granny Smith apple

Preparation:

1. Spread one side of both slices of whole grain bread with Dijon mustard. Assemble the panini by layering the cheddar cheese, ham, and apple slices in your preferred order between the bread slices, then lightly spray the outer sides of the bread with nonstick cooking spray. 2. Spray the fryer drawer with nonstick cooking spray, then place the sandwich in the drawer and cook at 150°C for 5 minutes or until the bread is toasted and the cheese melts. 3. Remove the panini from the fryer, place on a wire rack, and serve warm.

Chapter 1 Breakfast | 13

Christmas Pecan Eggnog Bread

⏰ **Prep: 10 minutes** 🍴 **Cook: 20 minutes** 📚 **Serves: 6**

Ingredients:

125g flour, plus more for dusting
45g sugar
1 teaspoon baking powder
¼ teaspoon salt
¼ teaspoon nutmeg
120ml eggnog
1 egg yolk
1 tablespoon butter, plus 1 teaspoon, melted
25g pecans
40g chopped candied fruit (cherries, pineapple, or mixed fruits)
Cooking spray

Preparation:

1. In a medium bowl, stir together the flour, sugar, baking powder, salt, and nutmeg. 2. Add eggnog, egg yolk, and butter. Mix well, but do not beat. 3. Stir in nuts and fruit. 4. Spray a round baking pan with cooking spray and dust with flour. 5. Spread batter into prepared pan and cook at 180°C for 20 minutes or until the top is dark golden brown and the bread just starts to pull away from the sides of the pan.

Cheese and Vegetable Frittata

⏰ **Prep: 15 minutes** 🍴 **Cook: 20 minutes** 📚 **Serves: 2**

Ingredients:

Cooking spray
4 large eggs
115g baby bella mushrooms, chopped
30g baby spinach, chopped
30g (from 1 large) chopped leek, white part only
55g shredded cheddar cheese
40g halved grape tomatoes
1 tablespoon semi-skimmed milk
½ teaspoon kosher salt
¼ teaspoon garlic powder
¼ teaspoon dried oregano
Freshly ground black pepper

Preparation:

1. Lightly spray a round baking dish with cooking spray. 2. In a large bowl, beat the eggs with a fork until uniform. Add the mushrooms, spinach, leek, cheddar, tomatoes, milk, salt, oregano, garlic powder, and black pepper to taste. Mix to combine and pour into the baking dish. 3. Place the pan in the air fryer drawer and cook at 150°C for 20 to 23 minutes until the eggs are set in the centre. 4. Cut the frittata in half and serve.

Chapter 1 Breakfast

Banana Blueberry Oatmeal Bake

⏰ Prep: 15 minutes　🍳 Cook: 25 minutes　📚 Serves: 4

Ingredients:
Cooking spray
2 large very ripe bananas (the riper the better)
105g quick-cooking oats (uncooked)
½ teaspoon baking powder
Pinch of kosher salt
120ml unsweetened almond milk (or any milk you desire)
5 tablespoons peanut butter powder
1 tablespoon honey
1 large egg
1 teaspoon vanilla extract
95g blueberries
4 tablespoons grape preserves

Preparation:
1. Generously spray a round cake pan with cooking spray. 2. In a medium bowl, mash the bananas well with a fork. In another medium bowl, stir together the oats, baking powder, and salt. 3. In a large bowl, whisk together the milk, peanut butter powder, honey, egg, and vanilla. Mix in the bananas until well incorporated, then add the oat mixture and combine. Fold in the blueberries. Pour into the prepared baking dish and spoon the jelly over the top by the teaspoon. 4. Place the baking dish in the air fryer drawer. Bake at 150°C for 25 minutes, or until the top is golden brown and the oatmeal is set in the centre. 5. Remove and set aside to cool for 10 to 15 minutes. Slice into 4 wedges and serve warm.

Butter Banana Bread

⏰ Prep: 5 minutes　🍳 Cook: 22 minutes　📚 Serves: 3

Ingredients:
3 ripe bananas, mashed
190g sugar
1 large egg
4 tablespoons (½ stick) unsalted butter, melted
185g all-purpose flour
1 teaspoon baking soda
1 teaspoon salt

Preparation:
1. Coat the insides of 3 mini loaf pans with cooking spray. 2. In a large mixing bowl, mix together the bananas and sugar. 3. In a separate large mixing bowl, combine the egg, butter, flour, baking soda, and salt and mix well. 4. Add the banana mixture to the egg and flour mixture. Mix well. 5. Divide the batter evenly among the prepared pans. 6. Set the mini loaf pans into the air fryer drawer. 7. Set the temperature to 155°C. Set the timer and bake for 22 minutes. 8. Insert a toothpick into the centre of each loaf; if it comes out clean, they are done. If the batter clings to the toothpick, cook the loaves for 2 minutes more and check again. 9. When the loaves are cooked through, use silicone oven mitts to remove the pans from the air fryer drawer. Turn out the loaves onto a wire rack to cool.

Bacon, Egg, and Cheese Breakfast Pockets

⏰ Prep: 20 minute   🍳 Cook: 20 minutes   ◈ Serves: 4

Ingredients:

Filling:
4 slices centre-cut bacon, chopped
50g diced red or green bell pepper
35g chopped scallions
4 large eggs
¼ teaspoon kosher salt
Freshly ground black pepper
30g shredded cheddar cheese

Dough:
140g all-purpose flour, plus more for dusting
1½ teaspoons baking powder
½ teaspoon kosher salt
245g fat-free Greek yoghurt (not regular yoghurt), drained of any liquid

Assembly and Serving:
1 large egg white, beaten
2 teaspoons "everything bagel" seasoning
Cooking spray
Hot sauce (optional)

Preparation:

For the filling: 1. Place the bacon in a cold medium skillet. Turn the heat to medium and cook until browned and crispy, about 4 to 5 minutes. Transfer to a plate lined with paper towels using a slotted spoon. Drain all but ½ tablespoon bacon fat from the pan. Add the bell pepper and scallions and cook, stirring occasionally, until soft, about 2 minutes. 2. Meanwhile, in a small bowl, beat the eggs with the salt and the pepper to taste. Add to the pan with the veggies and cook, stirring to scramble the eggs, until set, 2 to 3 minutes. Stir in the cheddar and remove from the heat. Set aside to cool while you make the dough.

For the dough: 1. In a medium bowl, combine the flour, baking powder, and salt and whisk well. Add the yoghurt and mix with a fork or spatula until well combined (it will look like small crumbles). 2. Lightly dust a work surface with flour. Transfer the dough to the work surface and knead for 2 to 3 minutes by hand until it is smooth and slightly tacky (it should not leave the dough on your hand). 3. Divide the dough into 4 equal balls. Dust the work surface and a rolling pin with flour. Roll each ball into a 7-inch round.

To assemble: 1. Divide the cooked egg-veggie-cheese mixture among the dough rounds, evenly spreading the filling over the bottom half of each and leaving a 1-inch border. Sprinkle each with one-quarter of the cooked bacon. 2. Brush the edges of the dough with the egg white and fold the top of the dough over the filling to make a half moon, leaving a ½-inch border uncovered at the bottom. Seal the edges by pinching the layers together or crimping them with a fork. Poke the top 4 or 5 times with a fork, then brush with the egg white. Sprinkle each with ½ teaspoon of the "everything bagel" seasoning. 3. Spray the bottom of the air fryer drawers with cooking spray to prevent sticking. Arrange a single layer of the pockets in each air fryer drawer. Select the Match Cook setting. Bake at 175°C for 6 minutes, then flip. Continue cooking for another 4 minutes or until golden. 4. Serve with hot sauce, if desired.

Perfect Cinnamon Rolls

⏰ **Prep: 45 minutes**　🍴 **Cook: 5 minutes**　◆ **Serves: 12**

Ingredients:

Dough:
60ml warm water (40–45°C)
1 teaspoon active dry yeast
1 tablespoon sugar
120ml buttermilk, lukewarm
250g flour, plus more for dusting
1 teaspoon baking powder
½ teaspoon salt
3 tablespoons cold butter

Filling:
1 tablespoon butter, melted
1 teaspoon cinnamon
2 tablespoons sugar

Icing:
80g powdered sugar
¼ teaspoon vanilla
2–3 teaspoons milk

Preparation:

1. Dissolve the yeast and sugar in warm water. Add buttermilk, stir, and set aside. 2. In a large bowl, sift together flour, baking powder, and salt. Using knives or a pastry blender, cut in the butter until the mixture is well combined and crumbly. 3. Pour in the buttermilk mixture and stir with a fork until a ball of dough forms. 4. Knead the dough on a lightly floured surface for 5 minutes. Roll into an 8 x 11-inch rectangle. 5. For the filling, spread the melted butter over the dough. 6. In a small bowl, mix together the cinnamon and sugar, then sprinkle over the dough. 7. Starting on a long side, roll up the dough so that you have a roll about 11 inches long. Cut into 12 slices with a serrated knife and sawing motion, so slices remain round. 8. Place rolls on a plate or cookie sheet about an inch apart and let rise for 30 minutes. 9. For icing, mix the powdered sugar, vanilla, and milk. Stir and add additional milk until the icing reaches a good spreading consistency. 10. Place 6 cinnamon rolls in each drawer and select the Match Cook setting. Cook at 180°C for 5 to 6 minutes or until the top springs back when lightly touched. Repeat to cook the remaining 6 rolls. 11. Spread icing over warm rolls and serve.

Homemade Bagels

⏲ **Prep: 15 minutes**   🍳 **Cook: 15 minutes**   ❖ **Serves: 4**

Ingredients:

140g unbleached all-purpose or whole wheat flour, plus more for dusting
2 teaspoons baking powder
¾ teaspoon kosher salt
245g fat-free Greek yoghurt (not regular yoghurt), drained of any liquid
1 egg white, beaten
Optional toppings: "everything bagel" seasoning (poppy seeds, sesame seeds, dried garlic flakes, and dried onion flakes) or any of your favourite bagel toppings

Preparation:

1. In a medium bowl, combine the flour, baking powder, and salt and whisk well. Add the yoghurt and mix with a fork or spatula until well combined (it will look like small crumbles). 2. Lightly dust a work surface with flour. Transfer the dough to the work surface and knead for 2 to 3 minutes by hand until it is smooth and slightly tacky (it should not leave the dough on your hand when you pull it away). Divide the dough into 4 equal balls. Roll each ball into a ¾-inch-thick rope and join the ends to form bagels. Brush the tops with the egg white and sprinkle both sides with a topping of your choice, if desired. 3. Place the 2 bagels in each air fryer drawer in a single layer. Select the Match Cook setting. Bake at 140°C for 15 to 16 minutes (no need to flip), until golden. Let cool for at least 15 minutes before cutting and serving.

Chapter 2 Vegetables and Sides

Roasted Lemon Broccoli

⏱ Prep: 10 minutes   🍳 Cook: 10 minutes   ⬢ Serves: 4

Ingredients:

1 large head fresh broccoli
2 teaspoons olive oil
1 tablespoon lemon juice

Preparation:

1. Rinse the broccoli and pat dry. Cut off the florets and separate them. You can use the stems of the broccoli, too; cut them into 1″ chunks and peel them. 2. Toss the broccoli, olive oil, and lemon juice in a large bowl until coated. 3. Roast the broccoli in the air fryer at 195°C for 10 to 14 minutes or until the broccoli is crisp-tender and slightly brown around the edges. Repeat with the remaining broccoli. Serve immediately.

Smashed Potatoes with Yoghurt and Tomatoes

⏱ Prep: 10 minutes   🍳 Cook: 20 minute   ⬢ Serves: 4

Ingredients:

24 small new potatoes, or creamer potatoes, rinsed, scrubbed, and patted dry
1 teaspoon olive oil
120g low-fat Greek yoghurt
1 tablespoon low-sodium stone-ground mustard
½ teaspoon dried basil
3 Roma tomatoes, seeded and chopped
2 scallions, white and green parts, chopped
2 tablespoons chopped fresh chives

Preparation:

1. In a large bowl, toss the potatoes with the olive oil. Transfer to the air fryer drawer. Roast at 180°C for 20 to 25 minutes, shaking the drawer once, until the potatoes are crisp on the outside and tender within. 2. Meanwhile, in a small bowl, stir together the yoghurt, mustard, and basil. 3. Place the potatoes on a serving platter and carefully smash each one slightly with the bottom of a drinking glass. 4. Top the potatoes with the yoghurt mixture. Sprinkle with the tomatoes, scallions, and chives. Serve immediately.

Crispy Shishito Tempura

⏰ Prep: 15 minutes   🍲 Cook: 8 minutes   ◆ Serves: 4

▶ **Ingredients:**

125g all-purpose flour
65g cornstarch
2 teaspoons baking soda
1 teaspoon kosher salt
240ml seltzer water or club soda
225g shishito peppers
Vegetable oil for spraying

▶ **Preparation:**

1. To make the tempura batter, whisk together the flour, cornstarch, baking soda, and salt in a large bowl. Gradually whisk in the seltzer water until a thick batter forms. Set a cooling rack on a board lined with wax or parchment paper. Using the stem as a handle, dip a shishito pepper in the batter, then tap it against the side of the bowl several times to remove any excess. Place the battered peppers on the rack. 2. Brush the drawer of the air fryer lightly with oil to prevent sticking. Arrange the battered peppers in a single layer in the air fryer drawer. Spray the peppers with oil. Cook at 180°C or 7 to 8 minutes until the peppers are browned on the outside and tender on the inside. (Do not be alarmed if you hear the peppers popping in the air fryer. This is normal.) 3. Remove the peppers from the air fryer and place on a serving plate or platter. Serve the peppers warm.

Crispy Corn Croquettes

⏰ Prep: 10 minutes   🍲 Cook: 12 minutes   ◆ Serves: 4

▶ **Ingredients:**

105g leftover mashed potatoes
310g corn kernels (if frozen, thawed, and well drained)
¼ teaspoon onion powder
⅛ teaspoon ground black pepper
¼ teaspoon salt
55g panko breadcrumbs
Oil for misting or cooking spray

▶ **Preparation:**

1. Place the potatoes and half the corn in a food processor and pulse until the corn is well chopped. 2. Transfer the mixture to a large bowl and stir in the remaining corn, onion powder, pepper and salt. 3. Shape the mixture into 16 balls. 4. Roll balls in panko crumbs, mist with oil or cooking spray, and place in air fryer drawer. 5. Cook at 180°C for 12 to 14 minutes, until golden brown and crispy.

Orange Honey Glazed Carrots

⏰ **Prep: 10 minutes** 🍲 **Cook: 10 minutes** ❖ **Serves: 4**

Ingredients:

2 teaspoons honey
1 teaspoon orange juice
½ teaspoon grated orange rind
⅛ teaspoon ginger
455g baby carrots
2 teaspoons olive oil
¼ teaspoon salt

Preparation:

1. Combine honey, orange juice, grated rind, and ginger in a small bowl and set aside. 2. Toss the carrots, oil, and salt together to coat well and pour them into the air fryer drawer. 3. Cook at 200°C for 5 minutes. Shake the drawer to stir a little and cook for 2 to 4 minutes more, until carrots are barely tender. 4. Pour carrots into an air fryer baking pan. 5. Stir the honey mixture to combine well, pour glaze over carrots, and stir to coat. 6. Cook at 180°C for 1 minute or just until heated through.

Spicy Brussels Sprouts

⏰ **Prep: 10 minutes** 🍲 **Cook: 15 minutes** ❖ **Serves: 4**

Ingredients:

680g Brussels sprouts, trimmed and, if large, halved
1 tablespoon extra-virgin olive oil
½ teaspoon salt
2 tablespoons maple syrup
3 tablespoons soy sauce
1 clove garlic, minced
Juice and zest of 1 lime
1 tablespoon sriracha

Preparation:

1. Toss the Brussels sprouts with the olive oil and salt. Using two drawers with the Match Cook setting, if necessary, arrange the sprouts in a single layer in the drawer of the air fryer. Cook at 190°C until browned, crispy, and fork-tender, 15 to 20 minutes. 2. While the Brussels sprouts are cooking, combine the soy sauce, maple syrup, lime zest and juice, garlic, and sriracha in a small saucepan. Bring to a boil over medium heat. Reduce the heat and simmer until thickened and slightly syrupy, 5 to 7 minutes. 3. Remove the Brussels sprouts from the air fryer. Place the Brussels sprouts in a serving bowl and drizzle the maple-soy sauce over them. Stir to coat the sprouts with the sauce and serve warm.

Chapter 2 Vegetables and Sides | 21

Prosciutto Wrapped Asparagus

⏱ **Prep: 10 minutes**   🍲 **Cook: 10 minutes**   ≋ **Serves: 4**

Ingredients:

12 asparagus spears, tough stems removed
6 thin slices prosciutto, each piece cut in half
15ml olive oil
½ teaspoon kosher salt
½ teaspoon black pepper

Preparation:

1. Carefully wrap 1 prosciutto piece around each asparagus spear. Drizzle with olive oil and sprinkle with salt and pepper. Arrange the asparagus spears in one layer in the air fryer drawer. 2. Cook at 180°C for 8 to 10 minutes or until the prosciutto is crispy and the asparagus is tender. Serve immediately.

Air Fryer Potatoes with Onions and Peppers

⏱ **Prep: 10 minutes**   🍲 **Cook: 35 minutes**   ≋ **Serves: 4**

Ingredients:

455g red potatoes, cut into ½-inch dice
1 medium onion, cut into ½-inch dice
1 large green bell pepper, cut into ½-inch dice
1 large red bell pepper, cut into ½-inch dice
1½ tablespoons extra-virgin olive oil
1¼ teaspoons kosher salt
¾ teaspoon garlic powder
¾ teaspoon sweet paprika
Freshly ground black pepper

Preparation:

1. In a large bowl, combine the potatoes, onion, bell peppers, oil, salt, garlic powder, paprika, and pepper to taste and toss well. 2. Add to the air fryer drawer in one batch. Cook at 175°C for about 35 minutes, shaking the drawer every 10 minutes, until the potatoes are golden brown and soft in the centre. Serve immediately.

Chapter 2 Vegetables and Sides

Cabbage and Mushroom Spring Rolls

⏰ Prep: 10 minutes   🍳 Cook: 7 minutes   🍽 Serves: 4

Ingredients:
1 tablespoon olive oil, divided
140g shredded cabbage
85g baby portobello mushrooms, chopped
1 teaspoon reduced-sodium soy sauce
4 egg roll wrappers

Preparation:
1. Place 1 teaspoon of olive oil in a small skillet and heat on medium-high, then add the cabbage, baby portobello mushrooms, and soy sauce. Sauté for 2 minutes. 2. Place 2 tablespoons of filling in the centre of an egg roll wrapper. Apply a small amount of water along the edges to help seal the wrapper, then fold in the sides and roll lengthwise. Repeat this process with the remaining wrappers, then brush the wrappers with the remaining 2 teaspoons of olive oil. 3. Spray the fryer drawer with nonstick cooking spray, then place the rolls in one layer in the drawer and cook at 180°C for 5–7 minutes or until golden brown. 4. Remove the spring rolls from the fryer and allow to cool on a wire rack for 5 minutes before serving.

Crispy Sweet Potato Fries with Curry Yoghurt Dip

⏰ Prep: 15 minutes   🍳 Cook: 13 minutes   🍽 Serves: 4

Ingredients:
Curry Yoghurt Dip:
230g plain Greek yoghurt, preferably full fat
60g mayonnaise
Juice of 1 lime
2 teaspoons curry powder, preferably muchi curry
Pinch each cayenne, cumin, coriander, garlic powder, and cinnamon
Sweet Potato Fries:
3 sweet potatoes, peeled and cut into ¼-inch (6 mm) batons
15ml vegetable oil
1 teaspoon kosher salt

Preparation:
1. To make the curry yoghurt dip, combine the Greek yoghurt and mayonnaise in a medium bowl. Add the lime juice and spices and whisk to combine. Cover and refrigerate for at least 1 hour prior to serving to allow the flavours to develop. 2. To make the sweet potato fries, toss the sweet potato batons with the oil and salt in a large bowl. Place a single layer of sweet potato fries in each drawer of the air fryer, taking care not to overcrowd the drawer. Select the Match Cook setting and cook at 180°C for 8 minutes, tossing the fries once halfway through. 3. Reduce the heat to 150°C and cook until the fries are well-browned and crispy, about 5 minutes. Serve the fries immediately with the curry yoghurt dip.

Chapter 2 Vegetables and Sides

Cinnamon Sweet Potato Slices

⏰ **Prep: 5 minutes**　🍲 **Cook: 8 minutes**　◆ **Serves: 6**

Ingredients:
1 small sweet potato, cut into ⅜-inch slices
Oil for misting
Ground cinnamon

Preparation:
1. Spray both sides of sweet potato slices with oil. Sprinkle both sides with cinnamon to taste. 2. Place potato slices in the air fryer drawer in a single layer. 3. Cook at 200°C for 4 minutes, turn, and cook for 4 more minutes or until potato slices are barely fork tender.

Chapter 2 Vegetables and Sides

Chapter 3 Snacks and Starters

Crispy Lime Avocado Fries

⏱ Prep: 5 minutes　🍳 Cook: 10 minutes　🍽 Serves: 4

Ingredients:

1 egg
1 tablespoon lime juice
⅛ teaspoon hot sauce
2 tablespoons flour
80g panko breadcrumbs
30g cornmeal
¼ teaspoon salt
1 large avocado
Oil for misting or cooking spray

Preparation:

1. In a small bowl, whisk together the egg, lime juice, and hot sauce. 2. Place flour on a sheet of wax paper. 3. Mix panko, cornmeal, and salt and place on another sheet of wax paper. 4. Split the avocado in half and remove the pit. Peel or use a spoon to lift avocado halves from the skin. 5. Cut avocado lengthwise into ½-inch slices. Dip each in flour, then egg wash, then roll in panko mixture. 6. Mist with oil or cooking spray and cook at 200°C for 10 minutes until the crust is brown and crispy.

Blooming Onion with Yum Yum Sauce

⏱ Prep: 15 minutes　🍳 Cook: 20 minutes　🍽 Serves: 4

Ingredients:

235ml aquafaba (from a 420g can of chickpeas)
60g all-purpose flour
¼ teaspoon kosher salt
55g seasoned breadcrumbs
1 large Vidalia onion

For the Sauce:
2 tablespoons vegan mayonnaise
2 tablespoons dairy-free plain yoghurt
2 tablespoons ketchup
1 to 2 teaspoons sriracha chilli sauce

Preparation:

1. Place the aquafaba in a medium shallow bowl. In a separate medium bowl, combine the flour, salt, and breadcrumbs. 2. Slice the top of the onion and turn it over to rest on a flat surface. Cut several slits around the entire onion, then turn it over and gently spread out the petals. Dip the onion in the aquafaba and then in the flour mixture. Sprinkle the flour mixture in between the petals and shake off any excess. Spray the onion with canola oil. 3. Place the onion in the fryer drawer and cook at 195°C until golden brown, about 20 to 22 minutes. 4. In a small bowl, make the yum yum sauce by whisking together the ingredients until smooth. 5. Transfer the blooming onion to a platter and serve immediately with the sauce.

Bacon-Wrapped Dates

⏰ **Prep: 10 minutes**　🍳 **Cook: 5 minutes**　📚 **Serves: 8**

Ingredients:

6 slices high-quality bacon, cut in half
12 dates, pitted

Preparation:

1. Wrap each date with half a bacon slice and secure with a toothpick. 2. Spray the fryer drawer with nonstick cooking spray, then place the bacon-wrapped dates in one layer in the drawer and cook at 180°C for 5–7 minutes or until the bacon is crispy. 3. Remove the dates from the fryer and allow to cool on a wire rack for 5 minutes before serving.

Mozzarella Sticks with Marinara Sauce

⏰ **Prep: 10 minutes**　🍳 **Cook: 5 minutes**　📚 **Serves: 4**

Ingredients:

25g panko breadcrumbs
2 tablespoons seasoned breadcrumbs
30g all-purpose flour
1 large egg, beaten
4 part-skim mozzarella cheese sticks
235ml marinara sauce

Preparation:

1. In a small bowl, combine the panko and seasoned breadcrumbs, then place the flour, egg, and breadcrumb mixture into 3 separate shallow bowls. 2. Cut the cheese sticks in half, dredge in the flour, then the egg, and finally the breadcrumb mixture. Place the coated sticks on a plate, then place the plate in the freezer for 10 minutes. 3. Place a piece of parchment paper on the bottom of the fryer drawer, then place the sticks on top. Cook at 180°C for 5–6 minutes or until crispy and golden brown. 4. Remove the mozzarella sticks from the fryer and allow to cool on a wire rack for 5 minutes before serving with the marinara sauce on the side for dipping.

Chapter 3 Snacks and Starters

Rosemary Roasted Cashews

⏰ Prep: 10 minutes 🍱 Cook: 3 minutes 🍽 Serves: 4

Ingredients:
2 sprigs of fresh rosemary (1 chopped and 1 whole)
1 teaspoon olive oil
1 teaspoon kosher salt
½ teaspoon honey
260g whole cashews, roasted and unsalted

Preparation:
1. In a medium bowl, whisk together the chopped rosemary, olive oil, kosher salt, and honey. Set aside. 2. Spray the fryer drawer with nonstick cooking spray, then place the cashews and the whole rosemary sprig in the drawer and cook at 150°C for 3 minutes. 3. Remove the cashews and rosemary from the fryer, then discard the rosemary and add the cashews to the olive oil mixture, tossing to coat. Allow to cool for 15 minutes before serving.

Spinach Artichoke Dip

⏰ Prep: 10 minutes 🍱 Cook: 10 minutes 🍽 Serves: 6

Ingredients:
1 (395g) can artichoke hearts packed in water, drained and chopped
1 (285g) package frozen spinach, thawed and drained
1 teaspoon minced garlic
2 tablespoons mayonnaise
60g non-fat plain Greek yoghurt
25g shredded part-skim mozzarella cheese
25g grated Parmesan cheese
¼ teaspoon freshly ground black pepper

Preparation:
1. Wrap the artichoke hearts and spinach in a paper towel and squeeze out any excess liquid, then transfer the vegetables to a large bowl. 2. Add the minced garlic, mayonnaise, plain Greek yoghurt, and mozzarella and Parmesan cheeses to the large bowl, stirring well to combine. 3. Spray a baking pan with nonstick cooking spray, then transfer the dip mixture to the pan and place it in the air fryer drawer. Cook at 180°C for 10 minutes. 4. Remove the dip from the fryer and allow to cool in the pan on a wire rack for 10 minutes before serving.

Chapter 3 Snacks and Starters | 27

Crunchy Chickpeas

⏰ **Prep: 5 minutes** 🍲 **Cook: 23 minutes** ◆ **Serves: 8**

Ingredients:

2 (425g) cans chickpeas
1 tablespoon olive oil
¼ teaspoon salt
¼ teaspoon pepper

Preparation:

1. Rinse and drain chickpeas; place on paper towels to absorb any excess water. Toss chickpeas, oil, salt, and pepper until evenly coated.
2. Place chickpeas in the air fryer drawer and air-fry at 200°C until crisp, 23 minutes, shaking the drawer twice. Remove from fryer and transfer to a bowl; toss with seasonings to your liking. Chickpeas will continue to crisp as they cool. Cool completely and store in an airtight container.

Crispy Kale Chips

⏰ **Prep: 10 minutes** 🍲 **Cook: 5 minutes** ◆ **Serves: 4**

Ingredients:

105g kale, large stems removed and chopped
2 teaspoons canola oil
¼ teaspoon smoked paprika
¼ teaspoon kosher salt

Preparation:

1. In a large bowl, toss the kale, canola oil, smoked paprika, and kosher salt. 2. Spray the fryer drawer with nonstick cooking spray, then place the kale in the drawer and cook at 200°C for 2–3 minutes. 3. Pause the fryer, shake the drawer, and cook for 2–3 more minutes or until crispy. 4. Remove the kale from the fryer and allow to cool on a wire rack for 3–5 minutes before serving.

Chapter 3 Snacks and Starters

Cheesy Stuffed Mushrooms

⏰ **Prep: 10 minutes**   🍱 **Cook: 10 minutes**   ❖ **Serves: 4**

Ingredients:

1 tablespoon olive oil
2 tablespoons grated Parmesan cheese
1 tablespoon fresh parsley, chopped
25g panko breadcrumbs
⅛ teaspoon freshly ground black pepper
8 baby portobello mushrooms, stems removed

Preparation:

1. In a large bowl, combine the olive oil, Parmesan cheese, parsley, panko breadcrumbs, and black pepper. 2. Spray the air fryer drawer with nonstick cooking spray, then spoon the filling into each baby portobello mushroom and place the mushrooms in the drawer. Cook at 180°C for 10 minutes or until tender. 3. Allow the mushrooms to cool in the pan in the fryer for 10 minutes. Serve warm.

Parmesan Cauliflower Cakes

⏰ **Prep: 10 minutes**   🍱 **Cook: 8 minutes**   ❖ **Serves: 4**

Ingredients:

280g cooked cauliflower
1 large egg, beaten
50g grated Parmesan cheese
1 tablespoon fresh chives, chopped
110g panko breadcrumbs

Preparation:

1. In a large bowl, combine the cauliflower, egg, Parmesan cheese, chives, and panko breadcrumbs, then use a potato masher to mash the ingredients, retaining a chunky texture. 2. Form the mixture into 6 round cakes, then spray both sides with nonstick cooking spray. 3. Spray the fryer drawers with nonstick cooking spray, then place 3 cakes in each drawer and select the Match Cook setting. Cook at 200°C for 8 minutes. 4. Remove the cakes from the fryer and allow to cool on a wire rack for 5 minutes before serving.

Chapter 3 Snacks and Starters

Shrimp Potstickers

⏱ **Prep: 30 minutes**   🍳 **Cook: 5 minutes**   ❖ **Serves: 10**

Ingredients:

225g peeled and deveined shrimp, finely chopped
1 medium courgette, coarsely grated (about 60g)
1 tablespoon green curry paste
1 tablespoon fish sauce
20g basil, chopped
2 scallions, thinly sliced
Round dumpling wrappers (about 30)
½ tablespoon canola oil
Oil in mister

Preparation:

1. Prepare filling: Stir together shrimp, courgette, curry paste, fish sauce, basil, and scallions. 2. Place 1 rounded teaspoon of the filling in the centre of 1 wrapper. Lightly moisten the edges of the wrapper with water using your fingers. Fold it in half and press to seal, pleating as desired. Transfer the sealed dumpling to a greased and floured or parchment-lined baking sheet. Repeat with the remaining filling and wrappers. 3. Combine ½ tablespoon oil and 60ml water in a small dish. Spray the air fryer drawer with oil. 4. Place the potstickers in one layer in the drawer and brush with oil-and-water mixture. Air-fry at 175°C until golden brown and crisp, 5 minutes. 5. Serve with Thai Lime Dipping Sauce (recipe below). Thai Lime Dipping Sauce: In a small bowl, stir together 1 tablespoon water, 1 tablespoon lime juice, 2 teaspoons fish sauce, 1 teaspoon low-sodium soy sauce, and 1 teaspoon green curry paste. Serve with potstickers.

Crisp Root Vegetable Chips

⏱ **Prep: 10 minutes**   🍳 **Cook: 8 minutes**   ❖ **Serves: 12**

Ingredients:

1 parsnip, washed
1 small beet, washed
1 small turnip, washed
½ small sweet potato, washed
1 teaspoon olive oil
For the Herb Salt:
¼ teaspoon kosher salt
2 teaspoons fresh parsley, finely chopped

Preparation:

1. Peel and thinly slice the parsnip, beet, turnip, and sweet potato, then place the vegetables in a large bowl, add the olive oil, and toss. 2. Spray the fryer drawer with nonstick cooking spray, then place the vegetables in the drawer and cook at 180°C for 8 minutes, pausing the fryer halfway through to gently shake the drawer. 3. While the chips cook, make the herb salt in a small bowl by combining the kosher salt and parsley. 4. Remove the chips from the fryer and place on a serving plate, then sprinkle the herb salt on top and allow to cool for 2–3 minutes before serving. (They'll become a little crisper as they cool.)

Chapter 4 Poultry

Honey-Lime Roasted Cornish Hen

⏱ Prep: 15 minutes   🍲 Cook: 25 minutes   ≡ Serves: 3

Ingredients:

1 Cornish game hen (680g–905g)
1 tablespoon honey
1 tablespoon lime juice
1 teaspoon poultry seasoning
Salt and pepper
Cooking spray

Preparation:

1. To split the hen into halves, cut through the breast bone and down one side of the backbone. 2. Mix the honey, lime juice, and poultry seasoning together and brush or rub onto all sides of the hen. Season to taste with salt and pepper. 3. Insert the grill plate in the air fryer drawer and spray with cooking spray. Place hen halves in the drawer, skin-side down. 4. Cook at 165°C for 25 to 30 minutes. The hen will be done when juices run clear when pierced at the leg joint with a fork. Let hen rest for 5 to 10 minutes before cutting.

Crispy Chicken Nuggets

⏱ Prep: 20 minutes   🍲 Cook: 13 minutes   ≡ Serves: 4

Ingredients:

455g boneless, skinless chicken thighs cut into 1-inch chunks
¾ teaspoon salt
½ teaspoon black pepper
½ teaspoon garlic powder
½ teaspoon onion powder
60g flour
2 eggs, beaten
55g panko breadcrumbs
3 tablespoons plain breadcrumbs
Oil for misting or cooking spray

Preparation:

1. In the bowl of a food processor, combine chicken, ½ teaspoon salt, pepper, garlic powder, and onion powder. Process in short pulses until chicken is very finely chopped and well blended. 2. Place flour in one shallow dish and beaten eggs in another. In a third dish or plastic bag, mix together the panko crumbs, plain breadcrumbs, and ¼ teaspoon salt. 3. Shape the chicken mixture into small nuggets. Dip nuggets in flour, then eggs, then panko crumb mixture. 4. Spray nuggets on both sides with oil or cooking spray and place in the air fryer drawer in a single layer, close but not overlapping. 5. Cook at 180°C for 10 minutes. Spray with oil and cook for 3 to 4 minutes, until chicken is done and coating is golden brown.

Crispy Chicken Tenderloins

⏰ Prep: 15 minutes   🍳 Cook: 12 minutes   🍽 Serves: 4

Ingredients:
8 chicken tenderloins
1 egg, beaten
2 tablespoons olive oil
110g breadcrumbs
Black pepper and salt to taste

Preparation:
1. Combine the friendly breadcrumbs, olive oil, salt and black pepper in a shallow dish. 2. Put the beaten egg in a separate dish. 3. Dip the chicken tenderloins into the egg before rolling them in the breadcrumbs. 4. Transfer to the Air Fryer drawer. Air fry the chicken at 175°C for 12 minutes.

Italian Sausage Calzones

⏰ Prep: 15 minutes   🍳 Cook: 12 minutes   🍽 Serves: 4

Ingredients:
250g part-skim ricotta cheese
1 link (85g) fully cooked Italian chicken sausage, diced
100g frozen peas
50g shredded part-skim mozzarella cheese
1 package (455g) refrigerated pizza dough
235ml marinara sauce, warmed

Preparation:
1. In a medium-sized bowl, stir together ricotta, sausage, frozen peas, and mozzarella. 2. Divide dough into 4 pieces. Using fingertips, press each piece of dough into a 7-inch-wide oval. 3. Place ¼ of the ricotta filling on half of each piece of dough. Brush the rim of the dough with water and fold the other half of the dough over the filling. Pinch edges together to seal. Repeat with the remaining filling and dough. 4. Place 2 calzones in each drawer and select the Match Cook setting. Air-fry at 180°C for 12 minutes or until browned and heated through, turning over halfway during cooking with tongs. 5. Serve with marinara sauce.

Italian Parmesan Chicken

⏱ Prep: 15 minutes   🍳 Cook: 10 minutes   🍽 Serves: 4

Ingredients:

2 (115g) boneless, skinless chicken breasts
110g Italian breadcrumbs
50g grated Parmesan cheese
2 teaspoons Italian seasoning
Salt
Black pepper
2 egg whites
Cooking oil
175ml marinara sauce
55g shredded mozzarella cheese

Preparation:

1. With your knife blade parallel to the cutting board, slice the chicken breasts in half horizontally to create 4 thin cutlets. 2. On a solid surface, pound the cutlets to flatten them. You can use your hands, a rolling pin, a kitchen mallet, or a meat hammer. 3. In a bowl large enough to dip a chicken cutlet, combine the breadcrumbs, Parmesan cheese, Italian seasoning, and salt and black pepper to taste. Stir to combine. 4. Pour the egg whites into another bowl large enough to dip the chicken. 5. Spray the air fryer drawer with cooking oil. 6. Dip each cutlet in the egg whites and then the breadcrumb mixture. 7. Place the chicken cutlets in a single layer in the air fryer drawer. Spray the top of the chicken with cooking oil. Cook at 185°C for 7 minutes. 8. Open the air fryer. Top the chicken cutlets with the marinara sauce and shredded mozzarella. Cook for an additional 3 minutes or until the cheese has melted. 9. Cool before serving.

Chicken Kabobs with Bell Peppers and Onions

⏱ Prep: 10 minutes   🍳 Cook: 15 minutes   🍽 Serves: 5

Ingredients:

4 (115g) boneless, skinless chicken breasts, cut into 1-inch cubes
Chicken seasoning or rub
Salt
Pepper
1 green bell pepper, seeded and cut into 1-inch pieces
1 red bell pepper, seeded and cut into 1-inch pieces
½ red onion, cut into 1-inch pieces
Cooking oil

Preparation:

1. Season the chicken with chicken seasoning, salt, and pepper to taste. 2. Thread wooden skewers with the cubed chicken, red bell pepper, green bell pepper, and onion. 3. Spray the air fryer drawer with cooking oil. 4. Insert the grill plate in the air fryer drawer and spray with cooking spray. Place the kabobs in the air fryer and do not overcrowd. Spray the kabobs with cooking oil. Cook at 180°C for 8 minutes. 5. Open the air fryer and flip the kabobs. Cook for an additional 7 minutes. 6. Remove the cooked kabobs from the air fryer. 7. Cool before serving.

Air Fryer Cajun Chicken Drumsticks

⏰ **Prep: 5 minutes**   🍲 **Cook: 18 minutes**   ❖ **Serves: 5**

Ingredients:

10 chicken drumsticks
1½ tablespoons Cajun seasoning
Salt
Pepper
Cooking oil

Preparation:

1. Season the drumsticks with the Cajun seasoning and salt and pepper to taste. 2. Spray the air fryer drawer with cooking oil. 3. Place the drumsticks in the air fryer. Do not stack. Spray the drumsticks with cooking oil. Cook at 200°C for 10 minutes. 4. Open the air fryer and flip the chicken. Cook for an additional 8 minutes. 5. Remove the cooked chicken from the air fryer. 6. Cool before serving.

Buttermilk Fried Chicken Wings

⏰ **Prep: 10 minutes**   🍲 **Cook: 20 minutes**   ❖ **Serves: 4**

Ingredients:

16 chicken wings
1 teaspoon garlic powder
Chicken seasoning or rub
Pepper
60g all-purpose flour
60ml low-fat buttermilk
Cooking oil

Preparation:

1. Place the chicken in a sealable plastic bag. Add the garlic powder, then add chicken seasoning or rub and pepper to taste. Seal the bag. Shake the bag thoroughly to combine the seasonings and coat the chicken. 2. Pour the flour into a second sealable plastic bag. 3. Pour the buttermilk into a bowl large enough to dunk the chicken. One at a time, dunk the wings in the buttermilk, then place them in the bag of flour. Seal and shake to thoroughly coat the chicken. 4. Spray the air fryer drawer with cooking oil. 5. Using tongs, transfer the chicken from the bag to the air fryer drawer. It is okay to stack the wings on top of each other. Spray the chicken with cooking oil, being sure to cover the bottom layer. Cook at 200°C for 5 minutes. 6. Remove the drawer and shake it to ensure all of the chicken pieces will cook fully. 7. Return the drawer to the air fryer and continue to cook the chicken. Repeat shaking every 5 minutes until 20 minutes have passed. 8. Cool before serving.

Hot and Spicy Chicken Wings

Prep: 10 minutes   Cook: 24 minutes   Serves: 4

Ingredients:

8 tablespoons (1 stick) unsalted butter, melted
120ml hot sauce
2 tablespoons white vinegar
2 teaspoons Worcestershire sauce
1 teaspoon garlic powder
60g all-purpose flour
16 frozen chicken wings

Preparation:

1. In a small saucepan over low heat, combine the butter, hot sauce, vinegar, Worcestershire sauce, and garlic. Mix well and bring to a simmer. 2. Pour the flour into a medium mixing bowl. Dredge the chicken wings in the flour. 3. Place the flour-coated wings into the air fryer drawer. 4. Set the timer and fry at 185°C for 12 minutes. 5. Using tongs, flip the wings. 6. Reset the timer and fry for 12 minutes more. 7. Put the chicken wings into a large mixing bowl, then pour the sauce over them. 8. Serve and enjoy!

Cheesy Chicken Taquitos

Prep: 15 minutes   Cook: 6 minutes   Serves: 6

Ingredients:

1 teaspoon butter
2 tablespoons chopped green onions
225g cooked chicken, shredded
2 tablespoons chopped green chillis
55g Pepper Jack cheese, shredded
4 tablespoons salsa
½ teaspoon lime juice
¼ teaspoon cumin
½ teaspoon chilli powder
⅛ teaspoon garlic powder
12 corn tortillas
Oil for misting or cooking spray

Preparation:

1. Melt butter in a saucepan over medium heat. Add green onions and sauté a minute or two, until tender. 2. Remove from heat and stir in the chicken, green chillies, cheese, salsa, lime juice, and seasonings. 3. To soften refrigerated tortillas, wrap them in damp paper towels and microwave for 35 to 55 seconds until slightly warmed. 4. Remove one tortilla at a time, keeping others covered with damp paper towels. Place a heaping tablespoon of filling into a tortilla, roll it up and secure with a toothpick. Spray all sides with oil or cooking spray. 5. Place taquitos in the air fryer drawer, either in a single layer or stacked. To stack, leave plenty of space between taquitos and alternate the direction of the layers, 6 on the bottom lengthwise, then 6 more on top crosswise. 6. Cook at 200°C for 4 to 6 minutes or until brown and crispy. 7. Serve hot with guacamole, sour cream, salsa.

Chapter 4 Poultry

Turkey Cheeseburgers

⏱ **Prep: 5 minutes**   🍲 **Cook: 12 minutes**   ⬧ **Serves: 4**

Ingredients:

455g ground turkey
40g diced red onion
1 tablespoon grilled chicken seasoning
½ teaspoon dried parsley
½ teaspoon salt
4 slices provolone cheese
4 whole-grain sandwich buns
Suggested toppings: lettuce, sliced tomatoes, dill pickles, and mustard

Preparation:

1. Combine the turkey, onion, chicken seasoning, parsley, and salt and mix well. 2. Shape into 4 patties. 3. Cook at 180°C for 9 to 11 minutes or until turkey is well done and juices run clear. 4. Top each burger with a slice of cheese and cook for 1 to 2 minutes to melt. 5. Serve on buns with your favourite toppings.

Turkey and Rice Stuffed Poblano Peppers

⏱ **Prep: 15 minutes**   🍲 **Cook: 11 minutes**   ⬧ **Serves: 4**

Ingredients:

2 large poblano peppers (approx. 5½ inches long excluding stem)
340g ground turkey, raw
150g cooked brown rice
1 teaspoon chilli powder
½ teaspoon ground cumin
½ teaspoon garlic powder
115g sharp Cheddar cheese, grated
1 225g jar salsa, warmed

Preparation:

1. Slice each pepper in half lengthwise so that you have four wide, flat pepper halves. 2. Remove seeds and membrane and discard. Rinse inside and out. 3. In a large bowl, combine turkey, rice, chilli powder, cumin, and garlic powder. Mix well. 4. Divide turkey filling into 4 portions and stuff one into each of the 4 pepper halves. Press lightly to pack down. 5. Place the pepper halves in the air fryer drawer and cook at 200°C for 10 minutes or until turkey is well done. 6. Top each pepper half with ¼ of the grated cheese. Cook 1 more minute or just until the cheese melts. 7. To serve, place the pepper half on a plate and top with 60ml warm salsa.

| Chapter 4 Poultry

Buffalo Chicken Drumettes

⏰ **Prep: 10 minutes**   🍱 **Cook: 17 minutes**   ◈ **Serves: 6**

Ingredients:

16 chicken drumettes (party wings)
1 teaspoon garlic powder
Chicken seasoning or rub
Pepper
Cooking oil
60ml buffalo sauce

Preparation:

1. Season the drumettes with garlic powder, chicken seasoning, and pepper to taste. 2. Place the chicken in the air fryer drawer. It is okay to stack the drumettes on top of each other. Spray them with cooking oil. Cook for 5 minutes. 3. Remove the drawer and shake it to ensure all of the pieces will cook fully. Cook for an additional 5 minutes. 4. Open the air fryer and transfer the drumettes to a large bowl. Toss the drumettes with the Buffalo wing sauce, ensuring each is covered. 5. Return the drumettes to the air fryer. Cook for 7 minutes. 6. Cool before serving.

Herb Roasted Chicken Breast

⏰ **Prep: 15 minutes**   🍱 **Cook: 22 minutes**   ◈ **Serves: 4**

Ingredients:

4 chicken breasts, skinless and boneless
½ teaspoon dried oregano
½ teaspoon dried basil
½ teaspoon dried thyme
½ teaspoon garlic powder
2 tablespoons olive oil
⅛ teaspoon black pepper
½ teaspoon salt

Preparation:

1. In a suitable bowl, mix together olive oil, oregano, basil, thyme, garlic powder, black pepper, and salt. 2. Rub herb oil mixture all over chicken breasts. 3. Grease its air fryer drawer with cooking spray. 4. Place chicken in the air fryer drawer and cook at almost 180°C for almost 10 minutes. Flip the chicken and continue cooking for 8-12 minutes more or until the internal temperature of the chicken reaches 75°C. 5. Serve and enjoy.

Chapter 4 Poultry | 37

Parmesan Chicken with Roasted Peanuts

⏱ **Prep: 15 minutes**   🍲 **Cook: 13 minutes**   ❖ **Serves: 4**

▶ **Ingredients:**

680g chicken tenderloins
2 tablespoons peanut oil
50g parmesan cheese, grated
25g panko breadcrumbs
Salt and black pepper, to taste
½ teaspoon garlic powder
1 teaspoon red pepper flakes
2 tablespoons peanuts, roasted and roughly chopped

▶ **Preparation:**

1. Brush the chicken tenderloins with peanut oil on all sides. 2. In a suitable mixing bowl, thoroughly combine grated parmesan cheese, panko breadcrumbs, salt, black pepper, garlic powder, and red pepper flakes. 3. Dredge the chicken in the prepared breading, shaking off any residual coating. 4. Lay the chicken tenderloins into the cooking drawer. 5. Cook at 180°C for almost 12 to 13 minutes or until it is no longer pink in the centre. 6. Serve garnished with roasted peanuts.

Chinese Chicken with Broccoli

⏱ **Prep: 15 minutes**   🍲 **Cook: 20 minutes**   ❖ **Serves: 4**

▶ **Ingredients:**

455g chicken breast, skinless, boneless, and cut into chunks
180g broccoli florets
2 teaspoons hot sauce
2 teaspoons vinegar
1 teaspoon sesame oil
1 tablespoon soy sauce
1 tablespoon ginger, minced
½ teaspoon garlic powder
1 tablespoon olive oil
½ onion, sliced
Black pepper
Salt

▶ **Preparation:**

1. Add all the recipe ingredients into the suitable mixing bowl and toss well. 2. Grease its air fryer drawer with cooking spray. 3. Transfer the chicken and broccoli mixture into the air fryer drawer. 4. Cook at 195°C for 15-20 minutes. Shake halfway through. 5. Serve and enjoy.

Chapter 4 Poultry

Homemade Nacho Chicken Strips

⏰ **Prep: 20 minutes**　🍲 **Cook: 6 minutes**　📚 **Serves: 6**

Ingredients:

455g chicken tenders
Salt
60g flour
2 eggs
80g panko breadcrumbs
25g crushed organic nacho cheese tortilla chips
Oil for misting or cooking spray
Seasoning Mix:
1 tablespoon chilli powder
1 teaspoon ground cumin
½ teaspoon garlic powder
½ teaspoon onion powder

Preparation:

1. Stir together all seasonings in a small cup and set aside. 2. Cut chicken tenders in half crosswise, then cut into strips no wider than about ½ inch. 3. Salt chicken to taste. Place strips in a large bowl and sprinkle with 1 tablespoon of the seasoning mix. Stir well to distribute seasonings. 4. Add flour to chicken and stir well to coat all sides. 5. Beat eggs together in a shallow dish. 6. In a second shallow dish, combine the panko, crushed chips, and the remaining 2 teaspoons of seasoning mix. 7. Dip chicken strips in eggs, then roll in crumbs. Mist with oil or cooking spray. 8. Chicken strips will cook best if done in two batches. They can be crowded and overlapping a little but not stacked in double or triple layers. 9. Place the chicken strips in a single layer in the air fryer drawer. You can use two drawers with the Match Cook setting if necessary. Cook at 200°C for 4 minutes. Shake drawer, mist with oil, and cook 2 to 3 more minutes, until chicken juices run clear and the outside is crispy.

Chapter 5 Fish and Seafood

Parmesan Cod Fillets with Spring Onion

⏰ **Prep: 15 minutes**　🍲 **Cook: 14 minutes**　📚 **Serves: 4**

Ingredients:

4 cod fillets, boneless
Black pepper and salt to the taste
100g parmesan
4 tablespoons balsamic vinegar
A drizzle of olive oil
3 spring onions, chopped

Preparation:

1. Season fish with salt and black pepper, grease with the oil, and coat it in parmesan. 2. Put the fillets in one air fryer drawer and cook at 185°C for 14 minutes. 3. Meanwhile, in a suitable bowl, mix the spring onions with salt, black pepper and vinegar and whisk. 4. Divide the cod between plates, drizzle the spring onions, mix all over and serve with a side salad.

Old Bay Tilapia Fillets

⏰ **Prep: 15 minutes**　🍲 **Cook: 7 minutes**　📚 **Serves: 2**

Ingredients:

2 tilapia fillets
1 teaspoon Old Bay seasoning
½ teaspoon butter
¼ teaspoon lemon pepper
Black pepper
Salt

Preparation:

1. Grease the air fryer drawer with cooking spray. 2. Place prepared fish fillets into the air fryer drawer and season with lemon pepper, butter, old bay seasoning, black pepper, and salt. 3. Spray fish fillets with cooking spray and cook at 200°C for 7 minutes. 4. Serve and enjoy.

Crisp White Fish with Parsley

⏰ **Prep: 15 minutes** 🍲 **Cook: 12 minutes** ❖ **Servings: 4**

Ingredients:

70g crushed saltines
60ml extra-virgin olive oil
1 teaspoon garlic powder
½ teaspoon shallot powder
1 egg, well whisked
4 white fish fillets
Salt and black pepper to taste
Fresh Italian parsley to serve

Preparation:

1. In a shallow bowl, combine the crushed saltines and olive oil. 2. In a separate bowl, mix together the garlic powder, shallot powder, and the beaten egg. 3. Sprinkle a good amount of black pepper and salt over the fish before dipping each fillet into the egg mixture. 4. Coat the fillets with the crumb mixture. 5. Air fry the fish at 185°C for 10-12 minutes. 6. Serve with fresh parsley.

Salmon Croquettes

⏰ **Prep: 10 minutes** 🍲 **Cook: 8 minutes** ❖ **Serves: 4**

Ingredients:

1 tablespoon oil
55g breadcrumbs
1 420g can salmon, drained and all skin and fat removed
1 egg, beaten
25g coarsely crushed saltine crackers (about 8 crackers)
½ teaspoon Old Bay Seasoning
½ teaspoon onion powder
½ teaspoon Worcestershire sauce

Preparation:

1. In a shallow dish, mix oil and breadcrumbs until crumbly. 2. In a large bowl, combine the salmon, egg, cracker crumbs, Old Bay, onion powder, and Worcestershire. Mix well and shape into 8 small patties about ½-inch thick. 3. Gently dip each patty into breadcrumb mixture and turn to coat well on all sides. 4. Cook at 200°C for 7 to 8 minutes or until the outside is crispy and browned.

Chapter 5 Fish and Seafood

Air Fryer Shrimp Patties

⏱ **Prep: 15 minutes**   🍲 **Cook: 12 minutes**   ◆ **Serves: 4**

Ingredients:

225g shelled and deveined raw shrimp
35g chopped red bell pepper
40g chopped green onion
30g chopped celery
335g cooked sushi rice
½ teaspoon garlic powder
½ teaspoon Old Bay Seasoning
½ teaspoon salt
2 teaspoons Worcestershire sauce
55g plain breadcrumbs
Oil for misting or cooking spray

Preparation:

1. Finely chop the shrimp. You can do this in a food processor, but it takes only a few pulses. Be careful not to overprocess into mush. 2. Place shrimp in a large bowl and add all other ingredients except the breadcrumbs and oil. Stir until well combined. 3. Shape shrimp mixture into 8 patties, no more than ½-inch thick. Roll patties in breadcrumbs and mist with oil or cooking spray. 4. Place the shrimp patties in the air fryer drawer and cook at 200°C for 10 to 12 minutes, until the shrimp cooks through and the outside is crispy.

Crispy Coconut Shrimp

⏱ **Prep: 10 minutes**   🍲 **Cook: 8 minutes**   ◆ **Serves: 4**

Ingredients:

455g raw shrimp, peeled and deveined
1 egg
30g all-purpose flour
30g shredded unsweetened coconut
25g panko breadcrumbs
Salt
Pepper
Cooking oil

Preparation:

1. Dry the shrimp with paper towels. 2. In a small bowl, beat the egg. In another small bowl, place the flour. In a third small bowl, combine the coconut and panko breadcrumbs and season with salt and pepper to taste. Mix well. 3. Spray the air fryer drawer with cooking oil. 4. Dip the shrimp in the flour, then the egg, and then the coconut and breadcrumb mixture. 5. Place the shrimp in the air fryer drawer. It is okay to stack them. Cook at 200°C for 4 minutes. 6. Open the air fryer and flip the shrimp. I recommend flipping individually instead of shaking, which keeps the breading intact. Cook for an additional 4 minutes or until crisp. 7. Cool before serving.

Chapter 5 Fish and Seafood

Herbed Pollock with Olives and Tomatoes

Prep: 15 minutes　Cook: 13 minutes　Serves: 3

Ingredients:

2 tablespoons olive oil
1 red onion, sliced
2 garlic cloves, chopped
1 Florina pepper, deveined and minced
3 pollock fillets, skinless
2 ripe tomatoes, diced
12 Kalamata olives, pitted and chopped
2 tablespoons capers
1 teaspoon oregano
1 teaspoon rosemary
Salt, to taste
120ml white wine

Preparation:

1. Heat the oil in a suitable baking pan that fits your air fryer. 2. Once hot, sauté the onion, garlic, and black pepper for 2 to 3 minutes or until fragrant. Add the fish fillets to the baking pan. 3. Top with the tomatoes, olives, and capers. Sprinkle with the oregano, rosemary, and salt. 4. Pour in white wine and transfer to the cooking drawer. 5. Turn the temperature to 200°C and air fry for almost 10 minutes. 6. Enjoy!

Homemade Crunchy Shrimp

Prep: 1 hour 20 minutes　Cook: 8 minutes　Serves: 4

Ingredients:

455g (26–30 count) shrimp, peeled, deveined, and butterflied (last tail section of shell intact)
Marinade:
1 140g can evaporated milk
2 eggs, beaten
2 tablespoons white vinegar
1 tablespoon baking powder
Coating:
110g crushed panko breadcrumbs
½ teaspoon paprika
½ teaspoon Old Bay Seasoning
¼ teaspoon garlic powder
Oil for misting or cooking spray

Preparation:

1. Stir together all marinade ingredients until well-mixed. Add shrimp and stir to coat. Refrigerate for 1 hour. 2. Combine coating ingredients in a shallow dish. 3. Remove shrimp from marinade, roll in crumb mixture, and spray with olive oil or cooking spray. 4. Place shrimp in air fryer drawer in single layer, close but not overlapping. Cook at 200°C for 6 to 8 minutes, until light golden brown and crispy.

Chapter 5 Fish and Seafood | 43

Basil Tilapia with Garlic Aioli

⏰ **Prep: 5 minutes**　🍲 **Cook: 15 minutes**　◆ **Serves: 4**

Ingredients:

For the Tilapia:
4 tilapia fillets
1 tablespoon extra-virgin olive oil
1 teaspoon paprika
1 teaspoon garlic powder
1 teaspoon dried basil
Lemon-pepper seasoning

For the Garlic Aioli:
2 garlic cloves, minced
1 tablespoon mayonnaise
1 teaspoon extra-virgin olive oil
Juice of ½ lemon
Salt
Pepper

Preparation:

To make the tilapia: 1. Coat the fish with the olive oil. Season with the paprika, garlic powder, dried basil, and lemon-pepper seasoning. 2. Place the fish in the air fryer drawer. It is okay to stack the fish. Cook at 200°C for 8 minutes. 3. Open the air fryer and flip the fish. Cook for an additional 7 minutes.

To make the garlic aioli: 1. In a small bowl, combine the garlic, mayonnaise, olive oil, lemon juice, and salt and pepper to taste. Whisk well to combine. 2. Serve alongside the fish.

Spicy Lemon Shrimp

⏰ **Prep: 5 minutes**　🍲 **Cook: 8 minutes**　◆ **Serves: 4**

Ingredients:

455g raw shrimp, peeled and deveined
1 teaspoon paprika
½ teaspoon dried oregano
½ teaspoon cayenne pepper
Juice of ½ lemon
Salt
Black pepper
Cooking oil

Preparation:

1. Place the shrimp in a sealable plastic bag and add the paprika, oregano, cayenne pepper, lemon juice, salt and black pepper to taste. Seal the bag and shake well to combine. 2. Spray the air fryer drawer with cooking oil. 3. Place the shrimp in the air fryer. It is okay to stack the shrimp. Cook at 200°C for 4 minutes. 4. Open the air fryer and shake the drawer. Cook for an additional 3 to 4 minutes or until the shrimp has blackened. 5. Cool before serving.

Chapter 5 Fish and Seafood

Lemon-Herb Salmon

⏱ **Prep: 5 minutes**   🍳 **Cook: 10 minutes**   ❖ **Serves: 4**

Ingredients:

3 tablespoons unsalted butter
1 garlic clove, minced, or ½ teaspoon garlic powder
1 teaspoon salt
2 tablespoons freshly squeezed lemon juice
1 tablespoon minced fresh parsley
1 teaspoon minced fresh dill
1 teaspoon salt
½ teaspoon freshly ground black pepper
4 (115g) salmon fillets

Preparation:

1. Line the air fryer drawer with parchment paper. 2. In a small microwave-safe mixing bowl, combine the butter, garlic, salt, lemon juice, parsley, dill, salt, and pepper. 3. Place the bowl in the microwave and cook on low until the butter is completely melted, about 45 seconds. 4. Meanwhile, place the salmon fillets in the parchment-lined air fryer drawer. 5. Spoon the sauce over the salmon. 6. Set the temperature to 200°C. Set the timer and cook for 10 minutes. Since you don't want to overcook the salmon, begin checking for doneness at about 8 minutes. Salmon is done when the flesh is opaque and flakes easily when tested with a fork.

Stuffed Courgettes with Cheesy Tuna

⏱ **Prep: 15 minutes**   🍳 **Cook: 20 minutes**   ❖ **Serves: 4**

Ingredients:

4 medium courgette
120g of tuna in oil, canned drained
30g grated cheese
1 teaspoon pine nuts
Salt and black pepper to taste

Preparation:

1. Cut the courgette in ½ laterally and empty it with a small spoon. Set aside the pulp that will be used for filling; place them in the drawer. 2. Place the courgette pulp, drained tuna, pine nuts, and grated cheese in a food processor. 3. Mix until you get a homogeneous and dense mixture. Fill the courgette. 4. Air fry at 180°C for 20 minutes, depending on the size of the courgette. Let cool before serving.

Chapter 5 Fish and Seafood

Dill Salmon Patties

⏱ **Prep: 5 minutes**   🍲 **Cook: 10 minutes**   ❖ **Serves: 4**

Ingredients:

1 (420g) can wild salmon, drained
1 large egg
40g diced onion
55g breadcrumbs
1 teaspoon dried dill
½ teaspoon freshly ground black pepper
1 teaspoon salt
1 teaspoon Old Bay seasoning

Preparation:

1. Spray the air fryer drawer with olive oil. 2. Put the salmon in a medium bowl and remove any bones or skin. 3. Add the egg, onion, breadcrumbs, dill, pepper, salt, and Old Bay seasoning and mix well. 4. Form the salmon mixture into 4 equal patties. 5. Place the patties in the greased air fryer drawer. 6. Set the temperature to 185°C. Set the timer and grill for 5 minutes. 7. Flip the patties. Reset the timer and grill the patties for 5 minutes more. 8. Plate, serve, and enjoy!

Spicy Parmesan Tilapia

⏱ **Prep: 15 minutes**   🍲 **Cook: 10 minutes**   ❖ **Serves: 4**

Ingredients:

455g tilapia fillets
75g parmesan cheese, grated
1 tablespoon parsley, chopped
2 teaspoons paprika
1 tablespoon olive oil
Black pepper and salt to taste

Preparation:

1. In a shallow dish, combine together the paprika, grated cheese, black pepper, salt and parsley. 2. Pour a little olive oil over the tilapia fillets. 3. Cover the fillets with the paprika and cheese mixture. 4. Lay the fillets on a sheet of aluminium foil and transfer them to the Air Fryer drawer. 5. Air fry at 200°C for 10 minutes. Serve hot.

Chapter 5 Fish and Seafood

Lemon Butter Cod Fillets

⏰ Prep: 5 minutes 🍲 Cook: 12 minutes 🍽 Serves: 2

Ingredients:

2 (225g) cod fillets, cut to fit into the air fryer drawer
1 tablespoon Cajun seasoning
½ teaspoon lemon pepper
1 teaspoon salt
½ teaspoon freshly ground black pepper
2 tablespoons unsalted butter, melted
1 lemon, cut into 4 wedges

Preparation:

1. Spray the air fryer drawer with olive oil. 2. Place the fillets on a plate. 3. In a small mixing bowl, combine the Cajun seasoning, lemon pepper, salt, and pepper. 4. Rub the seasoning mix onto the fish. 5. Place the cod into the greased air fryer drawer. Brush the top of each fillet with melted butter. 6. Set the temperature to 180°C. Set the timer and cook for 6 minutes. 7. After 6 minutes, open up your air fryer drawer and flip the fish. Brush the top of each fillet with more melted butter. 8. Reset the timer and bake for 6 minutes more. 9. Squeeze fresh lemon juice over the fillets.

Crispy Fish Sticks

⏰ Prep: 20 minutes 🍲 Cook: 8 minutes 🍽 Serves: 4

Ingredients:

For the Sticks:
455g fish fillets
½ teaspoon hot sauce
1 tablespoon coarse brown mustard
1 teaspoon Worcestershire sauce
Salt
Crumb Coating:
80g panko breadcrumbs
30g stone-ground cornmeal
¼ teaspoon salt
Oil for misting or cooking spray

Preparation:

1. Cut fish fillets crosswise into slices 1-inch wide. 2. Mix the hot sauce, mustard, and Worcestershire sauce together to make a paste and rub on all sides of the fish. Season to taste with salt. 3. Mix the crumb-coating ingredients together and spread on a sheet of wax paper. 4. Roll the fish fillets in the crumb mixture. 5. Spray all sides with olive oil or cooking spray and place in the air fryer drawer in a single layer. 6. Cook at 200°C for 6 to 9 minutes until the fish flakes easily.

Chapter 5 Fish and Seafood

Chapter 6 Beef, Pork, and Lamb

Tender Rib Eye Steak

⏰ Prep: 15 minutes   🍳 Cook: 14 minutes   🍽 Servings: 2

Ingredients:
2 medium rib-eye steaks
¼ teaspoon garlic powder
¼ teaspoon onion powder
1 teaspoon olive oil
Black pepper
Salt

Preparation:
1. Coat steaks with oil and season with onion powder, garlic powder, black pepper, and salt. 2. Place steaks into the air fryer drawer and cook at 200°C for 14 minutes. Turn halfway through. 3. Serve and enjoy.

Savoury Meat Loaf

⏰ Prep: 10 minutes   🍳 Cook: 15 minutes   🍽 Serves: 4

Ingredients:
455g lean ground beef
2 large eggs, lightly beaten
160g diced yellow onion
5g chopped fresh coriander
1 tablespoon minced fresh ginger
1 tablespoon minced garlic
2 teaspoons Garam Masala
1 teaspoon kosher salt
1 teaspoon ground turmeric
1 teaspoon cayenne pepper
½ teaspoon ground cinnamon
⅛ teaspoon ground cardamom

Preparation:
1. In a large bowl, gently mix the ground beef, eggs, onion, coriander, ginger, garlic, garam masala, salt, turmeric, cayenne, cinnamon, and cardamom until thoroughly combined. 2. Place the seasoned meat in a round baking pan. Place the pan in the air-fryer drawer. Set the air fryer to 175°C for 15 minutes. Use a meat thermometer to ensure the meatloaf has reached an internal temperature of 70°C (medium). 3. Drain the fat and liquid from the pan and let stand for 5 minutes before slicing. 4. Slice and serve hot.

Air Fryer Steak Bites with Mushrooms

⏰ **Prep: 15 minutes** 🍲 **Cook: 18 minutes** ❖ **Serves: 3**

Ingredients:

455g steaks, cut into ½-inch cubes
½ teaspoon garlic powder
1 teaspoon Worcestershire sauce
2 tablespoon butter, melted
225g mushrooms, sliced
Black pepper
Salt

Preparation:

1. Add all the recipe ingredients into the suitable mixing bowl and toss well. 2. Grease its air fryer drawer with cooking spray. 3. Add steak mushroom mixture into the air fryer drawer and Cook at 200°C for 15-18 minutes. Shake the drawer twice. 4. Serve and enjoy.

Simple Beef Roast

⏰ **Prep: 15 minutes** 🍲 **Cook: 35 minutes** ❖ **Servings: 7**

Ingredients:

905g beef roast
1 tablespoon olive oil
1 teaspoon thyme
2 teaspoons garlic powder
¼ teaspoon black pepper
1 tablespoon kosher salt

Preparation:

1. Coat roast with olive oil. 2. Mix together thyme, garlic powder, black pepper, and salt and rub all over the roast. 3. Place roast into the air fryer drawer and Cook at 200°C for 20 minutes. 4. Spray roast with cooking spray and cook for 15 minutes more. 5. Slice and serve.

BBQ Pulled Pork Empanadas

⏰ **Prep: 10 minutes**　🍳 **Cook: 25 minutes**　❖ **Serves: 4**

Ingredients:

170g pork tenderloin
Kosher salt
Freshly ground black pepper
2 tablespoons spicy BBQ sauce
225g prepared pie crust

Preparation:

1. Spray the fryer drawer with nonstick cooking spray and season the pork with salt and black pepper, then place the pork in the drawer. Cook at 180°C for 20 minutes or until the internal temperature reaches 60°C. 2. Remove from the fryer and allow to cool on a wire rack for 10 minutes. (Clean the drawer while the pork cools.) 3. Once the pork has cooled, finely shred it, then combine the pork and BBQ sauce in a medium bowl. 4. Roll out the pie crust and cut out eight 4-inch-diameter circles, then place individual tablespoons of pork in the centre of each piece. Gently fold the dough over, creating a pocket, and use a fork to crimp the edges closed and a knife to poke a small hole in the top of each empanada to allow steam to escape. 5. Spray the fryer drawer with nonstick cooking spray, then place the empanadas in each drawer and cook at 200°C for 5 minutes or until golden brown. 6. Remove the empanadas from the fryer and allow to cool on a wire rack for 5 minutes before serving.

Spiced Sirloin Steak

⏰ **Prep: 7 minutes**　🍳 **Cook: 8 minutes**　❖ **Serves: 4**

Ingredients:

2 tablespoons low-sodium salsa
1 tablespoon minced chipotle pepper
1 tablespoon apple cider vinegar
1 teaspoon ground cumin
⅛ teaspoon freshly ground black pepper
⅛ teaspoon red pepper flakes
340g sirloin tip steak, cut into 4 pieces and gently pounded to about ⅓ inch thick

Preparation:

1. In a small bowl, thoroughly mix the salsa, chipotle pepper, cider vinegar, cumin, black pepper, and red pepper flakes. Rub this mixture into both sides of each steak piece. Let stand for 15 minutes at room temperature. 2. Place the steaks in in each drawer and cook at 200°C for 6 to 9 minutes, or until they reach at least 60°C on a meat thermometer. 3. Slice the steaks thinly against the grain and serve.

Spicy Garlic Lamb Chops

⏰ Prep: 15 minutes 🍳 Cook: 15 minutes 🍽 Serves: 4

Ingredients:

½ yellow onion, coarsely chopped
4 coin-size slices peeled fresh ginger
5 garlic cloves
1 teaspoon Garam Masala
1 teaspoon ground fennel
1 teaspoon ground cinnamon
1 teaspoon ground turmeric
½ to 1 teaspoon cayenne pepper
½ teaspoon ground cardamom
1 teaspoon kosher salt
455g lamb sirloin chops

Preparation:

1. In a blender, combine the onion, ginger, garlic, garam masala, fennel, cinnamon, turmeric, cayenne, cardamom, and salt. Pulse until the onion is finely minced and the mixture forms a thick paste, 3 to 4 minutes. 2. Place the lamb chops in a large bowl. Slash the meat and fat with a sharp knife several times to allow the marinade to penetrate better. Add the spice paste to the bowl and toss the lamb to coat. Marinate at room temperature for 30 minutes or cover and refrigerate for up to 24 hours. 3. Place the lamb chops in a single layer in the air-fryer drawer. Set the air fryer to 160°C for 15 minutes, turning the chops halfway through the cooking time. Use a meat thermometer to ensure the lamb has reached an internal temperature of 60°C (medium-rare).

Beef Steak Fajita Tacos

⏰ Prep: 15 minutes 🍳 Cook: 15 minutes 🍽 Serves: 4

Ingredients:

225g flank steak, sliced
¼ teaspoon ground cumin
¼ teaspoon kosher salt
¼ teaspoon chilli powder
1 red onion, sliced
1 green bell pepper, sliced
40g tomato, chopped
2 tablespoons fresh coriander, chopped
Squeeze of lime juice
4 six-inch corn tortillas

Preparation:

1. Place the steak in a large bowl, then add the cumin, kosher salt, and chilli powder, tossing to coat. 2. Spray the fryer drawer with nonstick cooking spray, then place the red onion and green bell pepper in the drawer, place the meat on top, and cook at 200°C for 15 minutes. 3. Remove the fajita mixture from the fryer, place it on a serving plate, and let cool for 5–10 minutes. Serve on corn tortillas, then top with the tomato, coriander, and a squeeze of lime juice.

Crispy Pork Belly

⏰ **Prep: 10 minutes**   🍲 **Cook: 15 minutes**   ❖ **Serves: 4**

Ingredients:
455g pork belly
710ml water
6 garlic cloves
2 tablespoons soy sauce
1 teaspoon kosher salt
1 teaspoon black pepper
2 bay leaves

Preparation:
1. Cut the pork belly into three thick chunks so it will cook more evenly. 2. Place the pork, water, garlic, soy sauce, salt, black pepper, and bay leaves in the inner pot of an Instant Pot or other electric pressure cooker. Seal and cook at high pressure for 15 minutes. Let the pressure release naturally for 10 minutes, then manually release the remaining pressure. (If you do not have a pressure cooker, place all the ingredients in a large saucepan. Cover and cook over low heat until a knife can be easily inserted into the skin side of pork belly, about 1 hour.) Using tongs, very carefully transfer the meat to a wire rack over a rimmed baking sheet to drain and dry for 10 minutes. 3. Cut each chunk of pork belly into two long slices. Arrange the slices in the air-fryer drawer. Set the air fryer to 200°C for 15 minutes or until the fat has crisped. 4. Serve immediately.

Easy Air Fried Hot Dogs

⏰ **Prep: 5 minutes**   🍲 **Cook: 6 minutes**   ❖ **Serves: 4**

Ingredients:
4 bun-length hot dogs
4 hot dog buns
Toppings, to your liking

Preparation:
1. Place hot dogs in the air fryer drawer. Air-fry at 200°C for 6 minutes or until lightly browned and heated. 2. Serve on a bun with a topping of your choice.

| Chapter 6 Beef, Pork, and Lamb

Beef Satay with Peanut Sauce

⏰ **Prep: 15 minutes**   🍳 **Cook: 7 minutes**   ◆ **Serves: 4**

Ingredients:

4 bamboo skewers, cut in half
225g London broil, sliced into 8 strips
2 teaspoons curry powder
½ teaspoon kosher salt
For the Sauce:
2 tablespoons creamy peanut butter
1 tablespoon reduced-sodium soy sauce
2 teaspoons rice vinegar
1 teaspoon honey
1 teaspoon grated ginger

Preparation:

1. Soak the bamboo skewers in room temperature water for 20 minutes before using them to prevent them from burning in the air fryer. Set aside. 2. Season the London broil with curry powder and kosher salt, then thread the beef onto the skewers. 3. Spray the drawer with nonstick cooking spray, then place the skewers in the drawer and cook at 180°C for 5–7 minutes or until the beef is cooked as desired. 4. While the beef cooks, make the sauce in a medium bowl by whisking together the peanut butter, soy sauce, rice vinegar, honey, and ginger. 5. Remove the beef from the fryer and allow it to cool slightly in the pan on a wire rack before serving with the dipping sauce on the side.

Curried Lime Pork Satay

⏰ **Prep: 15 minutes**   🍳 **Cook: 12 minutes**   ◆ **Serves: 4**

Ingredients:

1 (455g) pork tenderloin, cut into 1½-inch cubes
40g minced onion
2 garlic cloves, minced
1 jalapeño pepper, minced
2 tablespoons freshly squeezed lime juice
2 tablespoons coconut milk
2 tablespoons unsalted peanut butter
2 teaspoons curry powder

Preparation:

1 In a medium bowl, mix the pork, onion, garlic, jalapeño, lime juice, coconut milk, peanut butter, and curry powder until well combined. Let stand for 10 minutes at room temperature. 2 With a slotted spoon, remove the pork from the marinade. Reserve the marinade. 3 Thread the pork onto about 8 bamboo or metal skewers. Insert the grill plate in the air fryer drawer and spray with cooking spray. Place the kabobs in the air fryer and do not overcrowd. Spray the kabobs with cooking oil. Cook at 195°C for 12 minutes, brushing once with the reserved marinade, until the pork reaches at least 60°C on a meat thermometer. Discard any remaining marinade. Serve immediately.

Pork Burgers

⏰ **Prep: 20 minutes** 🍳 **Cook: 8 minutes** ❖ **Serves: 4**

Ingredients:

120g Greek yoghurt
2 tablespoons low-sodium mustard, divided
1 tablespoon lemon juice
15g sliced red cabbage
30g grated carrots
455g lean ground pork
½ teaspoon paprika
35g mixed baby lettuce greens
2 small tomatoes, sliced
8 small low-sodium whole-wheat sandwich buns, cut in half

Preparation:

1. In a small bowl, combine the yoghurt, 1 tablespoon of mustard, lemon juice, cabbage, and carrots; mix and refrigerate. 2. In a medium bowl, combine the pork, remaining 1 tablespoon mustard, and paprika. Form into 8 small patties. 3. Put the sliders into the air fryer drawer. Cook at 200°C for 7 to 9 minutes, or until the sliders register 75°C as tested with a meat thermometer. 4. Assemble the burgers by placing some of the lettuce greens on a bun bottom. Top with a tomato slice, the burgers, and the cabbage mixture. Add the bun top and serve immediately.

The Best Meatballs

⏰ **Prep: 10 minutes** 🍳 **Cook: 15 minutes** ❖ **Serves: 6**

Ingredients:

1 medium onion, minced
2 garlic cloves, minced
1 teaspoon olive oil
1 slice low-sodium whole-wheat bread, crumbled
3 tablespoons skimmed milk
1 teaspoon dried marjoram
1 teaspoon dried basil
455g lean ground beef

Preparation:

1. In a 6-by-2-inch pan, combine the onion, garlic, and olive oil. Air-fry at 195°C for 2 to 4 minutes or until the vegetables are crisp-tender. 2. Transfer the vegetables to a medium bowl, and add the breadcrumbs, milk, marjoram, and basil. Mix well. 3. Add the ground beef. With your hands, work the mixture gently but thoroughly until combined. Form the meat mixture into about 24 (1-inch) meatballs. 4. Arrange the meatballs evenly in the air fryer drawers. Select the Match Cook setting and cook at 195°C for 12 to 17 minutes, or until they reach 70°C on a meat thermometer. Serve immediately.

| Chapter 6 Beef, Pork, and Lamb

Meatballs with Creamy Gravy

⏰ **Prep: 25 minutes**   🍲 **Cook: 20 minutes**   📚 **Serves: 4**

Ingredients:

For the Meatballs:
80g fresh breadcrumbs
60ml heavy cream
40g finely chopped onion
½ teaspoon dried parsley flakes
½ teaspoon kosher salt
¼ teaspoon ground allspice
¼ teaspoon freshly grated nutmeg
¼ teaspoon white pepper
225g lean ground beef
225g ground pork
1 large egg, beaten
1 egg white, lightly beaten

For the Gravy:
2 tablespoons salted butter
2 tablespoons all-purpose flour
355ml low-sodium beef broth
1 teaspoon Worcestershire sauce
60ml heavy cream
Kosher salt and black pepper

For Serving:
Chopped fresh parsley
Lingonberry jam

Preparation:

1. For the meatballs: In a large bowl, mix the breadcrumbs and cream until well combined; let stand for 5 minutes. Add the onion, parsley flakes, salt, allspice, nutmeg, and white pepper. Stir to make a thick paste. Add the ground beef, ground pork, egg, and egg white. Mix until evenly combined. 2. Form into 1-inch meatballs. Place in a single layer in the air-fryer drawer. Set the air fryer to 175°C for 20 minutes, turning halfway through the cooking time. 3. Meanwhile, for the gravy: In a medium saucepan, melt the butter over medium heat. Add the flour and cook, whisking, until smooth. Whisk in the broth and Worcestershire. Bring to a simmer. Add the cream. Reduce the heat to medium-low and simmer until the gravy thickens, about 10 minutes. Season with salt and black pepper. 4. At the end of the cooking time, use a meat thermometer to check that the meatballs have reached an internal temperature of 70°C (medium). 5. Transfer the meatballs to a serving bowl. Ladle the gravy over the meatballs and sprinkle with parsley. Serve with lingonberry jam.

Delicious Turkish Pizza

⏱ Prep: 20 minutes   🍲 Cook: 10 minutes   ❖ Serves: 4

Ingredients:

115g ground lamb or lean ground beef
35g finely chopped green bell pepper
5g chopped fresh parsley
1 small plum tomato, seeded and finely chopped
2 tablespoons finely chopped yellow onion
1 garlic clove, minced
2 teaspoons tomato paste
¼ teaspoon sweet paprika
¼ teaspoon ground cumin
⅛ to ¼ teaspoon red pepper flakes
⅛ teaspoon ground allspice
⅛ teaspoon kosher salt
⅛ teaspoon black pepper
4 (6-inch) flour tortillas

For Serving:
Chopped fresh mint
Extra-virgin olive oil
Lemon wedges

Preparation:

1. In a medium bowl, gently mix the ground lamb, bell pepper, parsley, chopped tomato, onion, garlic, tomato paste, paprika, cumin, red pepper flakes, allspice, salt, and black pepper until well combined. 2. Divide the meat mixture evenly among the tortillas, spreading it all the way to the edge of each tortilla. 3. Place two tortillas in each air-fryer drawer and select the Match Cook setting. Set the air fryer to 200°C for 10 minutes, or until the meat topping has browned and the edge of the tortilla is golden. Transfer to a plate. Serve the pizzas warm, topped with chopped fresh mint and a drizzle of extra-virgin olive oil and with lemon wedges alongside.

Cheese Beef Lasagna

⏱ **Prep: 15 minutes**   🍲 **Cook: 20 minutes**   ❖ **Serves: 4**

Ingredients:

For the Meat Layer:
Extra-virgin olive oil
455g lean ground beef
235ml prepared marinara sauce
30g diced celery
40g diced red onion
½ teaspoon minced garlic
Kosher salt and black pepper

For the Cheese Layer:
225g ricotta cheese
95g shredded mozzarella cheese
50g grated Parmesan cheese
2 large eggs
1 teaspoon dried Italian seasoning, crushed
½ teaspoon each minced garlic, garlic powder, and black pepper

Preparation:

1. For the meat layer: Grease a 7½-inch barrel cake pan with 1 teaspoon olive oil. 2. In a large bowl, combine the ground beef, marinara, celery, onion, garlic, salt, and pepper. Place the seasoned meat in the pan. 3. Place the pan in the air-fryer drawer. Set the air fryer to 190°C for 10 minutes. 4. Meanwhile, for the cheese layer, in a medium bowl, combine the ricotta, half the mozzarella, the Parmesan, lightly beaten eggs, Italian seasoning, minced garlic, garlic powder, and pepper. Stir until well blended. 5. At the end of the cooking time, spread the cheese mixture over the meat mixture. Sprinkle with the remaining mozzarella. Set the air fryer to 190°C for 10 minutes or until the cheese is browned and bubbling. 6. At the end of the cooking time, use a meat thermometer to ensure the meat has reached an internal temperature of 70°C. 7. Drain the fat and liquid from the pan. Let stand for 5 minutes before serving.

Flavourful Vietnamese Roasted Pork

⏱ **Prep: 10 minutes**   🍲 **Cook: 20 minutes**   ❖ **Serves: 6**

Ingredients:

40g minced yellow onion
2 tablespoons sugar
2 tablespoons vegetable oil
1 tablespoon minced garlic
1 tablespoon fish sauce
1 tablespoon minced fresh lemongrass
2 teaspoons dark soy sauce
½ teaspoon black pepper
680g boneless pork shoulder, cut into ½-inch-thick slices
35g chopped salted roasted peanuts
2 tablespoons chopped fresh coriander or parsley

Preparation:

1. In a large bowl, combine the onion, sugar, vegetable oil, garlic, fish sauce, lemongrass, soy sauce, and pepper. Add the pork and toss to coat. Marinate at room temperature for 30 minutes, or cover and refrigerate for up to 24 hours. 2. Arrange the pork slices in the air-fryer drawer; discard the marinade. Set the air fryer to 200°C for 20 minutes, turning the pork halfway through the cooking time. 3. Transfer the pork to a serving platter. Sprinkle with the peanuts and coriander and serve.

Chapter 7 Desserts

Homemade Gingerbread

⏱ Prep: 5 minutes　🍳 Cook: 20 minutes　🍽 Serves: 6

Ingredients:

Cooking spray
125g flour
2 tablespoons sugar
¾ teaspoon ground ginger
¼ teaspoon cinnamon
1 teaspoon baking powder
½ teaspoon baking soda
⅛ teaspoon salt
1 egg
60ml molasses
120ml buttermilk
2 tablespoons oil
1 teaspoon pure vanilla extract

Preparation:

1. Spray a round baking dish lightly with cooking spray. 2. In a medium bowl, mix together all the dry ingredients. 3. In a separate bowl, beat the egg. Add molasses, buttermilk, oil, and vanilla and stir until well mixed. 4. Pour the liquid mixture into dry ingredients and stir until well blended. 5. Pour batter into the baking dish and cook at 165°C for 20 minutes or until a toothpick inserted in the centre of the loaf comes out clean.

Doughnuts with Chocolate Sauce

⏱ Prep: 5 minutes　🍳 Cook: 8 minutes　🍽 Serves: 8

Ingredients:

1 (225g) can jumbo biscuits
Cooking oil
Chocolate sauce, such as Hershey's

Preparation:

1. Separate the biscuit dough into 8 biscuits and place them on a flat work surface. Use a small circle cookie cutter or a biscuit cutter to cut a hole in the centre of each biscuit. You can also cut the holes using a knife. 2. Spray the air fryer drawers with cooking oil. 3. Place 4 doughnuts in each air fryer drawer. Do not stack. Spray with cooking oil. Cook at 180°C for 4 minutes. 4. Open the air fryer and flip the doughnuts. Cook for an additional 4 minutes. 5. Drizzle chocolate sauce over the doughnuts and enjoy while warm.

Cinnamon Doughnut Holes

⏰ **Prep: 5 minutes**　🍲 **Cook: 8 minutes**　📚 **Serves: 16**

Ingredients:
1 (225g) can jumbo biscuit dough
Cooking oil
1 tablespoon stevia
2 tablespoons cinnamon

Preparation:
1. Form the biscuit dough evenly into 16 balls, 1 to 1½ inches thick. 2. Spray the air fryer drawer with cooking oil. 3. Place 4 doughnut holes in each air fryer drawer. Do not stack. Spray them with cooking oil. Select the Match Cook setting. Cook at 180°C for 4 minutes. 4. Open the air fryer and flip the doughnut holes. Cook for an additional 4 minutes. 5. Allow the doughnut holes to cool. 6. In a small bowl, combine the stevia and cinnamon and stir. 7. Spritz the doughnut holes with cooking oil. Dip the doughnut holes in the cinnamon and sugar mixture, and serve.

Air Fried Pineapple Rings with Almonds

⏰ **Prep: 5 minutes**　🍲 **Cook: 12 minutes**　📚 **Serves: 4**

Ingredients:
Oil for misting or cooking spray
4 ½-inch-thick slices fresh pineapple, core removed
1 tablespoon honey
¼ teaspoon brandy
2 tablespoons slivered almonds, toasted
Vanilla frozen yoghurt or coconut sorbet

Preparation:
1. Spray both sides of pineapple slices with oil or cooking spray. Place directly into the air fryer drawer. 2. Cook at 200°C for 6 minutes. Turn slices over and cook for an additional 6 minutes. 3. Mix together the honey and brandy. 4. Remove cooked pineapple slices from the air fryer, sprinkle with toasted almonds, and drizzle with honey mixture. 5. Serve with a scoop of frozen yoghurt or sorbet on the side.

Chapter 7 Desserts

Sweet Coconut Rice Cake

⏱ **Prep: 8 minutes** 🍰 **Cook: 30 minutes** ❖ **Serves: 8**

Ingredients:

235ml all-natural coconut water
235ml unsweetened coconut milk
1 teaspoon almond extract
¼ teaspoon salt
4 tablespoons honey
Cooking spray
135g raw jasmine rice
280g sliced or cubed fruit

Preparation:

1. In a medium bowl, mix together the coconut water, coconut milk, almond extract, salt, and honey. 2. Spray the air fryer baking pan with cooking spray and add the rice. 3. Pour the liquid mixture over rice. 4. Cook at 180°C for 15 minutes. Stir and cook for 15 to 20 minutes longer or until rice grains are tender. 5. Allow the cake to cool slightly. Run a dull knife around the edge of the cake inside the pan. Turn the cake out onto a platter and garnish with fruit.

Classic Banana Bundt Cake

⏱ **Prep: 5 minutes** 🍰 **Cook: 30 minutes** ❖ **Serves: 4**

Ingredients:

60g brown sugar
4 tablespoons (½ stick) unsalted butter, at room temperature
1 ripe banana, mashed
1 large egg
2 tablespoons granulated sugar
125g all-purpose flour
1 teaspoon ground cinnamon
1 teaspoon vanilla extract
½ teaspoon ground nutmeg

Preparation:

1. Spray a 6-inch Bundt pan with cooking spray. 2. In a medium mixing bowl, cream the brown sugar and butter until pale and fluffy. 3. Mix in the banana and egg. 4. Add the granulated sugar, flour, ground cinnamon, vanilla, and nutmeg and mix well. 5. Spoon the batter into the prepared pan. 6. Place the pan in the air fryer drawer. 7. Set the temperature to 160°C. Set the timer and bake for 15 minutes. 8. Do a toothpick test. If the toothpick comes out clean, the cake is done. If there is batter on the toothpick, cook and check again in 5-minute intervals until the cake is done. It will likely take about 30 minutes total baking time to fully cook. 9. Using silicone oven mitts, remove the Bundt pan from the air fryer. 10. Set the pan on a wire cooling rack and let cool for about 10 minutes. Place a plate upside-down (like a lid) over the top of the Bundt pan. Carefully flip the plate and the pan over, and set the plate on the counter. Lift the Bundt pan off the cake. Frost as desired.

Chapter 7 Desserts

Fig and Almond Hand Pies

⏱ **Prep: 10 minutes**   🍳 **Cook: 5 minutes**   🍽 **Serves: 4**

Ingredients:
12 small flour tortillas (4-inch diameter)
160g fig preserves
25g sliced almonds
2 tablespoons shredded, unsweetened coconut
Oil for misting or cooking spray

Preparation:
1. Wrap refrigerated tortillas in damp paper towels and heat them in the microwave for 30 seconds to warm. 2. Working with one tortilla at a time, place 2 teaspoons fig preserves, 1 teaspoon sliced almonds, and ½ teaspoon coconut in the centre of each. 3. Moisten the outer edges of the tortilla all around. 4. Fold one side of the tortilla over filling to make a half-moon shape and press down lightly on the centre. Using the tines of a fork, press down firmly on the edges of the tortilla to seal in the filling. 5. Mist both sides with oil or cooking spray. 6. Place hand pies in the air fryer drawer close but not overlapping. It's fine to lean some against the sides and corners of the drawer. 7. Cook at 200°C for 5 minutes or until lightly browned. Serve hot. 8. Refrigerate any leftover pies in a closed container. To serve later, toss them back in the air fryer drawer and cook for 2 or 3 minutes to reheat.

Crispy Bananas with Chocolate Sauce

⏱ **Prep: 10 minutes**   🍳 **Cook: 7 minutes**   🍽 **Serves: 6**

Ingredients:
1 large egg
30g cornstarch
25g plain breadcrumbs
3 bananas, halved crosswise
Cooking oil
Chocolate sauce

Preparation:
1. In a small bowl, beat the egg. In another bowl, place the cornstarch. Place the breadcrumbs in a third bowl. 2. Dip the bananas in the cornstarch, then the egg, and then the breadcrumbs. 3. Spray the air fryer drawer with cooking oil. 4. Place the bananas in the drawer and spray them with cooking oil. Cook at 175°C for 5 minutes. 5. Open the air fryer and flip the bananas. Cook for an additional 2 minutes. 6. Transfer the bananas to plates. Drizzle the chocolate sauce over the bananas, and serve.

Chapter 7 Desserts

Chocolate Bundt Cake

⏰ Prep: 5 minutes   🍲 Cook: 30 minutes   🍽 Serves: 4

Ingredients:

220g all-purpose flour
375g sugar
65g unsweetened cocoa powder
1 teaspoon baking soda
1 teaspoon baking powder
120ml vegetable oil
1 teaspoon salt
2 teaspoons vanilla extract
2 large eggs
235ml milk
235ml hot water

Preparation:

1. Spray a 6-inch Bundt pan with cooking spray. 2. In a large mixing bowl, combine the flour, sugar, cocoa powder, baking soda, baking powder, oil, salt, vanilla, eggs, milk, and hot water. 3. Pour the cake batter into the prepared pan and set the pan in the air fryer drawer. 4. Set the temperature to 165°C. Set the timer and bake for 20 minutes. 5. Do a toothpick test. If the toothpick comes out clean, the cake is done. If there is batter on the toothpick, cook and check again in 5-minute intervals until the cake is done. It will likely take about 30 minutes total baking time to fully cook. 6. Using silicone oven mitts, remove the Bundt pan from the air fryer. 7. Set the pan on a wire cooling rack and let cool for about 10 minutes. Place a plate upside down (like a lid) over the top of the Bundt pan. Carefully flip the plate and the pan over, and set the plate on the counter. Lift the Bundt pan off the cake.

Easy Blueberry Crisp

⏰ Prep: 5 minutes   🍲 Cook: 15 minutes   🍽 Serves: 8

Ingredients:

80g rolled oats
60g all-purpose flour
60ml extra-virgin olive oil
¼ teaspoon salt
1 teaspoon cinnamon
80ml honey
Cooking oil
745g blueberries (thawed if frozen)

Preparation:

1. In a large bowl, combine the rolled oats, flour, olive oil, salt, cinnamon, and honey. 2. Spray a barrel pan with cooking oil all over the bottom and sides of the pan. 3. Spread the blueberries on the bottom of the barrel pan. Top with the oat mixture. 4. Place the pan in the air fryer. Cook at 175°C for 15 minutes. 5. Cool before serving.

Fudge Brownies

⏰ **Prep: 10 minutes**   🍲 **Cook: 20 minutes**   ◆ Serves: 6

Ingredients:

8 tablespoons (1 stick) unsalted butter, melted
190g sugar
1 teaspoon vanilla extract
2 large eggs
60g all-purpose flour
45g cocoa powder
1 teaspoon baking powder

Preparation:

1. Spray a 6-inch air fryer–safe baking pan with cooking spray or grease the pan with butter. 2. In a medium mixing bowl, mix together the butter and sugar, then add the vanilla and eggs and beat until well combined. 3. Add the flour, cocoa powder, and baking powder and mix until smooth. 4. Pour the batter into the prepared pan. 5. Set the temperature to 175°C. Set the timer and bake for 20 minutes. Once the centre is set, use silicon oven mitts to remove the pan from the air fryer. 6. Let cool slightly before serving.

Chapter 7 Desserts

Conclusion

As we reach the end of the Tower Dual Basket Air Fryer Cookbook, we hope you've found the inspiration to create delicious, healthy, and time-saving meals using your Tower Dual Basket Air Fryer. With its ability to cook multiple dishes at once, this appliance has undoubtedly transformed the way you approach everyday cooking, allowing you to prepare nutritious meals with ease and convenience.

The recipes in this cookbook have been designed to suit a wide range of tastes and dietary needs, making sure that there's something for everyone. From quick breakfasts to satisfying dinners, the Tower air fryer enables you to experiment with new flavours and techniques while cutting down on oil and fat, without compromising on taste or texture. Each recipe has been carefully crafted to help you get the most out of your air fryer, and we trust that the colour pictures have guided and inspired you along the way.

More than just a collection of recipes, this cookbook has also provided you with tips and tricks for making the most of the Tower Dual Basket Air Fryer, helping you achieve perfectly cooked meals every time. Whether you're new to air frying or an experienced home cook, we hope this guide has empowered you to explore all the possibilities this versatile appliance has to offer.

As you continue your journey with your Tower air fryer, we encourage you to revisit these recipes and experiment with your own creations. Cooking healthier meals has never been easier, and with the Tower Dual Basket Air Fryer, the possibilities are endless. Enjoy your culinary adventures and happy air frying!

Appendix Recipes Index

A
Air Fried Pineapple Rings with Almonds 60
Air Fryer Cajun Chicken Drumsticks 34
Air Fryer Potatoes with Onions and Peppers 22
Air Fryer Shrimp Patties 42
Air Fryer Steak Bites with Mushrooms 49

B
Bacon, Egg, and Cheese Breakfast Pockets 16
Bacon-Wrapped Dates 26
Banana Blueberry Oatmeal Bake 15
Basil Tilapia with Garlic Aioli 44
BBQ Pulled Pork Empanadas 50
Beef Satay with Peanut Sauce 53
Beef Steak Fajita Tacos 51
Blooming Onion with Yum Yum Sauce 25
Buffalo Chicken Drumettes 37
Butter Banana Bread 15
Buttermilk Fried Chicken Wings 34

C
Cabbage and Mushroom Spring Rolls 23
Cheese and Vegetable Frittata 14
Cheese Beef Lasagna 57
Cheesy Chicken Taquitos 35
Cheesy Ham and Tomato Sandwiches 12
Cheesy Stuffed Mushrooms 29
Chicken Kabobs with Bell Peppers and Onions 33
Chinese Chicken with Broccoli 38
Chocolate Bundt Cake 63
Christmas Pecan Eggnog Bread 14
Cinnamon Doughnut Holes 60
Cinnamon Sweet Potato Slices 24
Classic Banana Bundt Cake 61
Crisp Root Vegetable Chips 30
Crisp White Fish with Parsley 41
Crispy Bananas with Chocolate Sauce 62
Crispy Chicken Nuggets 31
Crispy Chicken Tenderloins 32
Crispy Coconut Shrimp 42
Crispy Corn Croquettes 20
Crispy Fish Sticks 47
Crispy Kale Chips 28
Crispy Lime Avocado Fries 25
Crispy Pork Belly 52
Crispy Shishito Tempura 20
Crispy Sweet Potato Fries with Curry Yoghurt Dip 23
Crunchy Chickpeas 28
Curried Lime Pork Satay 53

D
Delicious Turkish Pizza 56
Dill Salmon Patties 46
Doughnuts with Chocolate Sauce 59

E
Easy Air Fried Hot Dogs 52
Easy Blueberry Crisp 63
Egg in a Hole 11

F
Fig and Almond Hand Pies 62
Flavourful Vietnamese Roasted Pork 58
Fudge Brownies 64

H
Ham, Apple, and Cheddar Panini 13
Herb Roasted Chicken Breast 37
Herbed Pollock with Olives and Tomatoes 43
Homemade Bagels 18
Homemade Crunchy Shrimp 43
Homemade Gingerbread 59
Homemade Nacho Chicken Strips 39
Honey-Lime Roasted Cornish Hen 31
Hot and Spicy Chicken Wings 35

I
Italian Parmesan Chicken 33
Italian Sausage Calzones 32

L
Lemon Butter Cod Fillets 47
Lemon-Herb Salmon 45

M
Meatballs with Creamy Gravy 55
Mozzarella Sticks with Marinara Sauce 26

O
Old Bay Tilapia Fillets 40
Orange Honey Glazed Carrots 21

P
Parmesan Cauliflower Cakes 29
Parmesan Chicken with Roasted Peanuts 38
Parmesan Cod Fillets with Spring Onion 40
Perfect Cinnamon Rolls 17
Pork Burgers 54
Prosciutto Wrapped Asparagus 22

R
Roasted Lemon Broccoli 19
Rosemary Roasted Cashews 27

S
Salmon Croquettes 41
Savoury Meat Loaf 48
Shrimp Potstickers 30
Simple Beef Roast 49
Simple Breakfast Bread 12
Smashed Potatoes with Yoghurt and Tomatoes 19
Spiced Sirloin Steak 50
Spicy Brussels Sprouts 21
Spicy Garlic Lamb Chops 51
Spicy Lemon Shrimp 44
Spicy Parmesan Tilapia 46
Spinach Artichoke Dip 27
Stuffed Courgettes with Cheesy Tuna 45
Sweet Coconut Rice Cake 61

T
Tender Rib Eye Steak 48
The Best Meatballs 54
Tofu Breakfast Sandwich 13
Turkey and Rice Stuffed Poblano Peppers 36
Turkey Cheeseburgers 36

W
White Whole Wheat Walnut Bread 11

Printed in Great Britain
by Amazon